Mida

p.o. 68511

$57.95

BUSINESS DECISIONS, HUMAN CHOICES

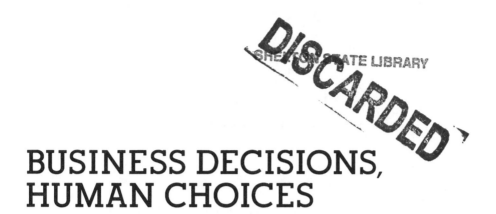

BUSINESS DECISIONS, HUMAN CHOICES

Restoring the Partnership Between
People and Their Organizations

Lloyd C. Williams

QUORUM BOOKS
Westport, Connecticut • London

Library of Congress Cataloging-in-Publication Data

Williams, Lloyd C.
    Business decisions, human choices : restoring the partnership
between people and their organizations / Lloyd C. Williams.
        p.   cm.
    Includes bibliographical references and index.
    ISBN 1–56720–015–X (alk. paper)
    1. Industrial management—Decision making.   2. Corporate culture.
3. Personnel management.   I. Title.
HD30.23.W537   1996
658.4'03—dc20   95–50740

British Library Cataloguing in Publication Data is available.

Library of Congress Catalog Card Number: 95–50740
ISBN: 1–56720–015–X

First published in 1996

Quorum Books, 88 Post Road West, Westport, CT 06881
An imprint of Greenwood Publishing Group, Inc.

Printed in the United States of America

∞™

The paper used in this book complies with the
Permanent Paper Standard issued by the National
Information Standards Organization (Z39.48–1984).

10 9 8 7 6 5 4 3 2 1

COPYRIGHT ACKNOWLEDGMENTS

The author and publisher gratefully acknowledge the following for permission to reprint passages previously published:

Quotes on pp. 44 and 130–131 from Paulo Freire, *Pedagogy of the Oppressed*
(New York: Seabury Press, 1973). Copyright ©1970, 1993 by Paulo Freire.
Reprinted by permission of the Continuum Publishing Company.

To all the professionals in
Organizational Development,
Clinical and Counseling Psychology,
and the creators of business.
You have helped change the world.

CONTENTS

FIGURES AND TABLES

ACKNOWLEDGMENTS

So many people need to be recognized in helping me with this book. Some of the people know who they are, others have no idea how they have helped me in the development of new paradigms for impacting people and business.

I would like to first thank Tony Gebarowski. Rarely has one person so completely impacted how I look at the world. His commitment to helping me achieve dreams is critical to my success in the books.

I would like to thank my publisher, Eric Valentine. At a time when I was not sure that I would publish, he believed in me and my writings. I truly thank him for his support in the publishing of all four of my books.

I would like to thank my parents who continually transform as they enter the twilight of their lives. Also, my sons, Marc Vaughn Williams and Scott Shields Williams, who carry on the family tradition of inquisitiveness and development and have been inspirational and supportive.

There are five professionals who have been most supportive: Dr. Grant Venerable, president of Ventec Corporation and a philosopher of Science professor at San Francisco State University; Dr. Barbara Jackson, president of Jackson, Fields & Allen; Dr. Mary Curran and Dr. Elizabeth-Taylor Gerdes, professors of Organizational Development and Transformation at the California Institute of Integral Studies; and Dr. Russell Jennings, president of Change Management Resources in Phoenix, Arizona.

Finally, there are the students of the Masters of Arts in Business program and the Master of Organizational Development and Transformation program who have been critical in challenging theoretical and practical applications of the theories. You have each made a difference in my thinking, and I will always be grateful to you for your challenges.

One last group of persons have been special in the development of this book—to all my clients, past, present, and future—thank you! This has been an exploration in transformation. What a journey! I am glad it is not over!

INTRODUCTION

In the other books that I have written, others have been kind enough to write introductions for the thoughts and values of the book to be read. This is written by me because this book has been so long in coming and I believe that I am the best person to tell you about it in a short space. The book is about transformation. Transformation is often a scary term, or at the least, an abstract term that eludes people and causes them to avoid reading the missals that follow. I hope you instead embrace this transformational process, taking it to heart as a strategy for real change in your personal and professional life.

The book is about reframing how one looks at business and the partnerships that businesses truly have with their employees and communities. Businesses are living entities. Living because how they choose to operate impacts the nature of human understanding for the employee and the nature of value to a community. Businesses are living metaphors for all beliefs and views within a community and a society. Businesses thrive because communities find value in the services and products interjected into the society. Businesses continue because the cultures of the communities sense that their lives are made better by the impact business has created in how they embrace the world. Businesses therefore become major vortexes in the creation and movement of the world.

Businesses have enormous responsibility, yet they often discount and take lightly their responsibility to all of us. I think there is a rational explanation for the sadness created by the actions of business in our current culture. That rational explanation is based on the paradigms that business use to make choices and decisions. Businesses in today's culture think in fragments. Businesses in today's culture compartmentalize their actions, seeing them as separate acts, often without impact on other actions of the corporate culture. Businesses have good intentions, yet often have devastating impacts.

This is a book that looks at altering the paradigms operational in business with a particular interest toward blending the needs of business and people in a tripartite system of collaboration and development. We are all impacted by the experiences we have, and most of us have experienced holocausts in our lives from our experiences with business. Trauma, pain, depression, violence, and sometimes psychosis have been the unfortunate outcomes of our experiences with business. I hope this book begins to help change that impact, creating options and opportunities for people and businesses to be better than they have in the past.

This book looks at the impacts of current business first. The first four chapters address topics of organizational and personal psychosis, manic–depressive behaviors created by organizational history and organizational action, organizational codependence, reactions, strategies for survival, and blame/shame processes as the controllers of personal performance within organizations. I looked at the clients and the staffs of organizations as I developed a framework for understanding current action.

As I described what disempowers and frustrates employees, I also began to address what can make a difference. Essential to that perspective was the realization that three primary factors were critical. The sense of humanity and its value in organizational process was important. The underlying paradigms and assumptions that framed the values and beliefs of organizations was important. Finally, the process by which organizations operate was important. What had not been done before was the development of a system that blended all three factors in an intentional strategy. This is a book about the creation of a new strategy. The change for business is attentiveness to all three factors in order to achieve success, not a haphazard approach to each "when it is convenient."

There are no easy answers for business; but there are consistent, congruent, and holistic strategies that can make a difference in the business process.

Chapter 1 is entitled "Dysfunctions in Choice: The Case for Organizational Makeovers." Societally, we have gone down a path that has bred greed, avarice, sabotage, competition, organizational restructures, and constant change without real attention to the impacts of those actions. The chapter focuses on the types of choices we make and what happens because of our choices.

Chapter 2 focuses on the internal political process and organizational history and how that history impacts leader decision making and the creation of organizational psychosis. Issues of thought, affect, perception, sense of self, volition, and responsibility all impact the politicizing of the decision-making process and the creation of additional dysfunctions.

Chapter 3 looks at the organizational history and fear components that often drive decision making with an explanation of how those actions impact the loss of organizational spirit. As organizations lose spirit, they begin to lose life. The depressive nature of the people and systems becomes the forefront of organizational action.

Chapter 4 looks at the actions of organizations in their attempts to create homogeneity. Irrespective of culture inclusions, when organizations demand that persons operate from a particular paradigm without expressed dialogue and inclusion in crafting or understanding the paradigm, dysfunctions occur. Issues of conduct disorders and oppositional defiant disorders become mainstays of the organization.

Chapter 5 focuses on the nature of organizational and personal shame, the culture of shame, and the adjustments we make in reaction to the actions of organizations and people. Chapter 6 focuses on organizational codependence and the commonness of the activity within organization. Control becomes a critical impact of the organizational action. The factors make the concept of living business anathemas to development and long-term growth. These chapters make up the first part of the book.

Chapter 7 begins the heart of the transformational process with the development and discussion of the creation of parallel paradigms. Some discussion occurs on paradigms in general and the necessity for the creation of parallel paradigms that focus on process versus ends and products as outcomes of organizational action. People development and business development create dual systems and those dual systems help move toward changing the paradigm of business. Focus is on the values that drive business and people and how those values can be conscious factors in personal and organizational decision making.

Chapter 8 talks of the use of the parallel paradigms and how organizations can move from closed systems to open systems. Key to this chapter is creation of new business philosophies and a step-by-step approach to changing business thinking. This is important if one is to later alter business action toward valuing community and people.

Chapter 9 is the most critical chapter of the book for it frames the integration of all that has gone before into the creation of the *trinity process*. The trinity process is the development of the tripartite system to focus on humanity, spirit, and context as the necessary strategy for understanding and actualizing business for the present and the future. This is an extremely important chapter, for it gives hope and strategy for changing and stopping the cycles currently in operation that disempower business and cause businesses to fail.

Chapters 10, 11, and 12 are examples of the utilization of the trinity process and a case study of its use currently being applied. This has been a difficult book, but I hope a very important one for the change of business for the future.

Enjoy your reading and call if I can be of assistance. This has been a wonderful exploration of change.

Asanté.

PART I

ORGANIZATIONAL DETACHMENTS: HOW WE CREATE OUR FRAGMENTS

DYSFUNCTIONS IN CHOICE

CHAPTER 1

The Case for Organizational Makeovers

Over the past twenty years, a change has occurred in organizations that has reframed the dynamics of successful business. From the early 1900s to the 1970s, a partnership existed between business leaders and their employees that allowed business success to live long and prosper. That success was based on respect, initiation, creation, and agreement about how work was accomplished, who would perform that work, and what work needed to occur. In the 1970s, a change began to emerge. Business schools began to prosper, finance became a driving force, and profit was the decision-making arm of organizational choices. During the past twenty years, the change in corporations and governments has caused a system of dysfunctions that has created new outcomes as by-products of organizational life that have been extremely unhealthy and destructive to organizational systems, people, and the perspectives of work, play, and community.

Our society has somehow embraced greed, avarice, sabotage, competition, downsizing, takeovers, staff reductions, organizational restructurings, and constant change of organizational mission as acceptable and appropriate for work life, albeit short-term oriented. In the wake of these organizational strategies, issues of people and families have decompensated to a level of dysfunction that suggests a makeover of the actions of organizations is at hand. Consider the following examples of organizational life that suggest an unhealthy and insane change. John Taylor is a facilities management manager at a psychiatric hospital in Hawaii. He has worked for the organization during the past fifteen years in the same capacity. In those years, he has never missed a day of work beyond his two-week vacation. He has believed in the organization and has committed to ensuring that the lights, power, and equipment always work effectively to ensure that the doctors, nurses, and administrators are always able to meet their outcomes within the organization. Recently, on a day that the hospital administrator reviewed the financial picture of the organization, she decided that the organization could save money by outsourcing the facilities management services. She called in John Taylor the next day, terminated his employment, and gave him two weeks severance. When the employees—psychiatrist, psychologist, psychiatric social workers, psychiatric nurses, secretaries, clerks, and janitors—heard of the situation, paranoia and fear set in. They were heard saying, "If this could happen to John, what about us?" Over the next three months, an exodus of good employees began to occur at the hospital. Doctors tried to develop strategies to get back to the mainland. Work productivity slowed down because the employees were more focused on their own lives than the success of the organization. Grant writing, special contracts with organizations to manage the health of the employees, and quality of care began to suffer. Within twelve months, the hospital was sold and all employees were displaced except the executive. She was transferred to the mainland to a new hospital. The announcement for her new appointment stated that she was an excellent money manger adept at ensuring the organization's fiscal health. And the cycle begins again.

Something is significantly wrong in our society when a bottom-line dollar figure allows choices to be made in the aforementioned manner. The situation of John Taylor can be recanted by thousands of loyal workers in our society who have given their professional life to an organization only to be replaced or displaced based on a figure in a line item of the organizational budget. Thousands of employees have been displaced every time an organizational board, shareholders, or leader determines that more profit is a valid rational marker for determining organizational decisions. No attempt was made to discuss with John Taylor other strategies that could reduce expenditures. No attempt was made to ask hospital personnel for their assistance in resolving the situation. Nor was any assessment made that addressed an outcome that was not based on money. John Taylor liked what he did for the organization and was extremely successful and dedicated to the organization's success. What has happened in a society where a set of figures on a balance sheet is *the* determining factor for organizational decision making? Is profit so essential in organizational life that destruction of people, creation of fear, and mistrust in other employees toward the organization and its leaders are acceptable business outcomes? What has happened to organizational leaders that makes these actions seem rational and appropriate in a society of people? Are these decisions that will play out in history as valid and sound business sense in the future? I do not think so.

This is a book about organizational mental health and choice. Too often, assessment of organizational life is made on the ability of the organization to achieve a profit or create a new product. Service is devalued or is valued at a cheaper cost. Critical to this discussion are the issues of compartmentalization, fragmentation, detachment, emotional intensity, and their impact on sound business decision making. Critical to this discussion is the awakening within the business leader, the human resource professional, the board member, and the business analyst a sense of humanity that has somehow been lost in the discussions at the decision-making tables in the ivory towers of America.

My father, Dr. T. S. Williams, was Dean of the School of Veterinary Medicine at Tuskegee Institute University for forty years. Throughout his professional life, I was always impressed with the choices and decisions that he made to ensure the survivability and emotional health of the school. He would agonize over the choices for systems versus people daily. He would meet with his peers, faculty, and students to develop strategies that impacted and balanced quality education and cost. There was a level of integrity and ethics in his decisions that made me proud of his choices. Over the forty years, there were painful times; however, most of the faculty remained and struggled with him to achieve the mission of quality veterinary medical education and fiscal health for the university. Each year in the annual symposiums, alumni return and generously give to the school to ensure its survivability, knowing that the school is committed to passionately and caringly responding to the needs of students, faculty, the university, and the community. A partnership among all the stakeholders has guided the direction of the school, and all the stakeholders have lived long and prospered. I am consistently struck by the inability or the lack of desire of organizations today to build partnerships with communities and the stakeholders of the organization. I am constantly struck by the discount of the employee as a key stakeholder. The words are always there, but the actions are a true disconnect with the words of the organization. This dissonance has caused me to view the actions of the organizations of our society as the makings of an ill mental health system.

This has probably caused you to say that the approach and concepts of this book are too avant garde for a business owner, business leader, business school professional, consultant, business student, or internal organizational professional to embrace. To the contrary, I believe that the issues of this book are the missing ingredient in organizational decision making. How we make choices, what we consider in those choices, the impacts of the decisions, how we compartmentalize our lives and our decisions, how we fragment the fabrics of professional and personal life, and how we detach our feelings from our decisions are exactly the issues that impact success in organizations and leading. We have too long disconnected who we are, how we think and feel, how we include, and how we find solutions as valid personal outcomes in business environments. If one only looks at the increase of weight, premature graying, and dreams that awaken us in the middle of the night, one can begin to sense that there is truth to the fact that we have participated in an emotional disconnect that harms and hurts the fabric of our personal and organizational being. As we think of those situations that have caused us trauma, we can begin to recognize the times in our professional lives that we have begun to detach our emotional selves, rationalizing our detachment as critical to business. As we re-experience those situations, we can sense the compartmentalization that occurs in our minds. Our brains push portions of pain to a corner that allows us to forget the damage we have experienced and participated in to justify decisions that harm in order to make a buck. We can sense the lack of emotional intensity that occurs in our lives when we are too tired to enjoy a child's recital or a child's new painting as we work at home in the office. We can sense that we are somehow disconnecting from all those important experiences that we claim we perform all this work to enjoy. We are participating in our own decompensation, and we rationalize our business decisions and our business choices saying that it is for the future. We have become delusional, dysfunctional, and "unable to tell the difference between fantasy and reality." We need organizational makeovers and we need to work toward the change more rapidly than we have thought in the past. Getting to it later is a perpetuation of the mental illness, and the costs continue to mount on a daily basis.

THE ISSUE OF CHOICE

Organizations will always seek strategies that allow alteration of the present to some definition of the future. The definitions of the future frame how an organization responds or reacts to issues of employment; organizational restructuring; policy changes; development; and implementation of societal imperatives such as domestic partners, workplace violence, compliance with drug testing laws, unfunded mandates from the federal government, stressors within the organization, or even new marketing techniques. Irrespective to the issues raised within organizational and personal life, the concept of choice is critical to the response or reaction created. Choice is the pivotal and ultimate point allowing people and systems to effectively move through the maze of rules, regulations, politics, and changes that impact overall success. As a consultant in therapeutic and organizational change, I am continually asked to guide managers, corporations, governments, and individuals to assess the efficacy of their choices. Politics, historical practice, family systems, and ethnic and cultural backgrounds are all factors that people and systems use to validate the choices that they make. The process of choice—outcomes of choice, dynamics of choice, tangents of choice, incidents of choice, and dissonance of choice—is key to making sound and holistic choices with organizational and personal buy-in. What is difficult is choosing without knowing. What is difficult is deciding from the perspectives of problems. What is dysfunctional is crafting decisions that place priority of one factor over another. In that process, the choice was never clear or accurate because the factors in the choice were not equal, and a level decision-making field never existed.

To effectively understand choices and their impact on organizational decision making, six types of choices need to be defined. Each type of choice has both a positive and a negative range for organizational and personal decision making. Part One of this book will focus on how fragmentation, compartmentalization, detachment, and emotional intensity often guide organizational and personal decision making. In each chapter of this section, a clinical dysfunction occurs. The framework for thinking is established to ask you to retool your process of examining and analyzing what happens around and to you as a leader, manager, employee, consultant, or teacher/student. Part Two looks at the impacts of the choice process in the creation of shaming strategies and blaming strategies within organizations. Part Three looks at what happens when our decision making focuses on incidents, tangents, and dissonance in the choice process to maintain the past, or what we know best with the concept of incremental change.

THE PROCESS OF CHOICE

The process of choice is a time continuum field of understanding the path of getting from point A to Z. As a friend once said, it is following both the bread crumbs and the pieces of the bread. Guiding principles and values are the initial framework for establishing congruence and consistency in the strategy developed to move from one historical place to another. As a consultant, if I value personal empowerment over organizational strategy, then each approach that I use to work with a client will start with an assessment of the empowerment levels of the people within the organization. I will sense that without the personal empowerment as a baseline for all organizational action, the organizational process will fail due to a discount of the people accountable for accomplishing the work within the organization. Conversely, I could be an executive that believes that a system of order is the underlying value for all decision making. With that perspective, all changes and choices must ensure that a system of order is in place. This approach might be in direct conflict with the previously stated process if I believe that order and empowerment are anathemas to movement from A to Z. Some theorists would call this a call to arms in adherence to an organizational value. I believe that this is deeper than that perspective. We all have values, we all have strategies, and we all have techniques that have worked for us in the past. We use them, yet rarely do we map out the process—the interrelationships that are essential to success. Emotions, feelings, beliefs, history, culture, gender, and traumas are factors that impact organizational and personal movement. These factors are considerations in choices, and they should become considerations in organizational decision making.

Where the process of change is selective and discounts all the factors essential in good decision making, the factors of clinical dysfunction begin to arise. Compartmentalization, fragmentation, and detachment become the key definers of process, and the lack of rational and sane steps begins to creep into the decision-making sphere. We often find ourselves stating that the employees do not understand, the managers are not team players, the board wants action, and that people will understand when we are through. This does not occur, however, and changes continue to mask the underlying issues that defeat the success of the decisions. More will be said of this process of choice in Chapters 2, 3, and 4.

DYNAMICS OF CHOICE

The dynamics of choice grow from the process of choice. Rather than addressing the factors of emotions, feelings, beliefs, history, culture, gender, and traumas, the dynamics of choice focus on the interrelationships prevalent in the strategies or patterns employed by the organization and the people in accomplishing outcomes. Usually within organizations, roles are played out to achieve an end. Gatekeepers, experts, protagonists, and so forth are roles that frame how work, or changes around the work, occur. If your role as a leader has always been to "lay something out there" for others to respond to, then change the direction based upon your reaction to the information received—you may be an antagonist in dynamics. This antagonistic process may radically determine how you make choices without the full effect of knowing the impact of your choices on organizational growth, change, and development. If you are an organization that has made it hard for people to risk, where risking is not valued and establishes blaming and shaming frameworks for risk, then you will find that the necessary dynamics of roles and strategies get hidden and withheld from sound, good information required for successful business decisions. Antagonism perpetuates the blaming process and defeats the potential for inclusion of others in the decision making. More will be said about this in Chapters 4, 5, and 6.

THE DISSONANCE OF CHOICE

The dissonance of choice is a sub-set component of the dynamics of choice. Dissonance speaks to what is out of whack and what is perceived differently by different people about the same issue. This is critical for leaders who often delude themselves into believing that organizational and personal buy-in has been achieved with stakeholders of systems. When the dynamics of change have gone awry, the dissonance of choice grows exponentially and people find themselves becoming more focused on protective and destructive strategies. Consider the following as an example.

George is the director of a manufacturing firm who never makes a firm decision. There is always room for change in the decision based on changing political winds or realistic new information. Unfortunately, this process of choice was never shared within the organization. Because of this strategy, the dynamics of choice within the organization have begun to shift. Where everyone used to perform varying roles, more and more roles have focused on protagonist and antagonist strategies with no gatekeepers or persons who ensure that all the pieces are in place and all the perspectives have been heard in developing a work process. Now the organization is faced internally with competitive- and sabotage-oriented behaviors that have created organizational and personal dissonance. The organization is fragmented, the staff is fragmented, and compartmentalization of different components of the work have become the norm. This fragmentation and compartmentalization leads to a cognitive dissonance around the work and the behaviors of the employees. George is oblivious to the impact of his process of choosing, but the consequences can destroy an organization.

THE TANGENTS OF CHOICE

Tangents of choice are strategies of compartmentalization. Where dissonance is a process of fragmentation, tangents are diversions that continually occur that cause leaders and decision makers to respond to issues from the tangential perspective. No straight paths exist in the process of tangents; there are always differing perspectives without connectors. Unfortunately, decision makers create decisions on little information and lots of nonconnecting points. Think of the times when you are confronted with numerous tangents—employees fighting in the yards, purchasing contracts have been violated, encumbrances of monies from one fiscal year to another were forgotten but contract work is occurring, your executive assistant is having an affair with the secretary and a sexual harassment suit has been filed, employees are complaining of compaction in the salary structure, ethnic groups in the community are complaining of disenfranchisement in the employee population of your company. You are likely to make the decision for each without consideration of the pattern within all of them. Reacting only to the presented information is making tangential decisions. There is a pattern here about the relationships and the communication process of this organization that might allow the decisions to take a significantly different twist for a true win-win among the stakeholders.

INCIDENTS OF CHOICE

Incidents of choice are the patterned actions internal to an organization that suggest that the choice made to resolve one situation was insufficient, causing the creation of a different incident to get a more rational decision made. Different from the tangents of choice that appear unconnected, the incidents of choice are very connected. Different players, different departments, different time periods, different locations—however amazingly similar—are incidents that suggest that choices must be congruent to truly resolve the actions in question. Issues of reflection, intuition, dialogue, sensing, and synergy are essential tools in the alteration of choices created by incidents.

Incidents define the emotional intensity of the organization and the persons within the organization. Where choices are made that enhance and move forward the life of the organization, the emotional intensity is high and focused toward positive and collaborative action. Where the choices restrict and turn back the life of the organization, emotional intensity is high but focused on competitive and sabotage-oriented action.

OUTCOMES OF CHOICE

Outcomes of choice are equally important to the process of choice. This is based on a reversal of so much theory in management, project management, and planning theories. In each of the aforementioned, there is a focus on the recognition and acknowledgment of knowing what the end must look like. For the purposes of effective decision making, focus here is on allowing the process to define the outcome and allowing the outcome to frame the strategies for the future. Appreciative inquiry is a process that comes to mind as an outcome choice approach that does not set parameters before one starts. Suresh Srivastva and David Cooperrider are the founders of this approach to change in their book, *Appreciative Management and Leadership.* In effect, the integration between self and work is essential because the life force of the organization guides the outcome rather than some incident, tangent, or predetermined product.

The outcomes of choice embody the life force of the decision-making process. The circle of process and outcome blend the true partnership essential to effective organizational decision making. The focus on tangents such as changes in the stock market, or on incidents such as continual loss of income in the manufacturing division of a paper company, is avoided in this process.

THE NEXT STEPS

How these truly impact the mental health of an organization is ultimately essential to a total understanding of the impact of choice on organizational functioning. Each chapter following builds that path with you to effective and healthy decision making.

ORGANIZATIONAL MAKEOVERS

The chapter is entitled, "Dysfunctions in Choice: The Case for Organizational Makeover." In twenty-five years of organizational management and the development of strategies for change, I am constantly confronted with the struggle to balance conventional strategies in business with the impacts of those strategies. The constant violence experienced with downsizing of companies, the leveraged buyouts, the re-engineering efforts for organizational health, the reactions of union struggles, and the potential revenge and sabotage of hurt employees never seem to awaken in the leaders of corporations the questions, "Have we gone too far? Is money too much of a driving force in our decision making? Have we consistently forced employees to justify their cost to the detriment of the product or service? Should business strive for a better balance—a balance of people and systems, of compassion and rigidness, of the gray areas of management and service—or is business on the right path?" I sense that business needs to take a different turn. Business must begin to squarely embrace the human factors, the sensual factors, and the emotional factors as legitimate components of business decision making. Leading by business school examples, organizational history, and the restrictions created in climbing the organizational ladder is not always the best model for leading. Relying on maintaining a level of unemployment in the United States as healthy for business is not always a sound model for effective decision making. Operating from political strategies rather than competency strategies is not an emotionally healthy perspective. Business needs a change.

Embark on the path of this book as a re-examination of your business and personal values and beliefs. Walk the talk that you have learned in trainings and espouse to your employees. Experience the frailty in the sincerity of the statements and the frustration in the reactions of the employees. Look at the strategies employed over and over again and recognize the continual trauma, pain, hurt, and mistrust evident in the actions of employees. Consider your own frustration as you believe you have acted in good faith for the good of the organization. Remember the responses you have received. Look at the reactions of the employees. Look at the hurt and pain, not the business decision. Think of how long it has taken you to be perceived as a fair and equitable manager and leader. Remember the reaction from that outspoken employee who said to you that you had no heart, that you were only in this for the money, and then think of your own pains as you climbed the ladder to success. Remember your choices to take different paths that got you to the top. If you can look at your past, remembering the pains, then maybe you can say that there is a better way, a holistic way, a more comprehensive way. Then say to yourself, maybe a totally new way is needed; maybe organizational makeover is right for my company and my employees now.

Your choices and decisions are not easy. Your desire to balance the need for profit and service with the needs of the employees is rarely understood. Your strategy often includes levels of organizational priority that staff is unaware of. Your decision is hard and you wish that people would walk in your shoes before they condemn you for your actions. You are right, they are right, the boards of directors are right, the community is right; and yet all of you are wrong, because the strategy employed is unhelpful and falls short of the desired outcome. We begin an understanding of these issues in Chapter 2.

POLITICS AS THE BASELINE OF CHOICE

CHAPTER

2

Impacts on Leader Decision Making and the Making of Organizational Psychosis

Joseph is the chief executive officer of a major water utility in the state of California. Joseph has been in the position for three years. He was brought to the utility to create change: change from a focus on technical issues in water to a focus on administrative management similar to the administration of city management. Joseph's focus was on sound fiscal management, downsized management, decentralized management, and effective decision making. Joseph was touted as the "consummate organizational change director." He quickly moved into the organization, challenging the lack of clear policies, centralized decision making, and rampant spending that seemed unfocused and inconsiderate of the needs of the rate payers. As the chief executive officer, he also believed that the organizational structure in place allowed too many people to have access to his time, defeating in his perspective the critical time he needed to make change. Joseph needed a new organizational structure. He brought in an external consultant and directed the consultant to develop a structure that reduced the number of direct reports from nine to four. The consultant, following directions, created a new tier in the organization of assistant executive officers, "to function as a policy team" and to ensure consistency and congruence in the organizational decision making and organizational process.

It all sounded so great. Employees were skeptical because all of the changes and the indictments were occurring within nine months of

Joseph's arrival as the organizational leader. Some initial observations from the employees were the inconsistencies in the statements from Joseph. He had stated that the new tier would not become "super department heads," but rather that they would allow access to the top for all employees of the organization. To the contrary, the three assistant executive officers were former city managers or city department directors, and they immediately structured their organizational entities as city departments reporting to them and creating an additional review cycle that slowed decision making, increased the workload, and increased the mistrust of the chief executive officer. A clear dissonance with the spoken word was evident in the choices made by the executive team.

Over a period of three years, the water utility had become a very dysfunctional organization. Employees were angry, mistrustful of management, forming unions, stalling work, searching for new careers, praying and wishing that the executive team would disappear, and longing for the days of old where an executive made a decision, stuck to his guns, and valued them as important pieces of accomplishing work and serving the rate payers. Employees were attacking each other, searching for strategies of survival, and focusing on political movement rather than professional competence. Employees were taking on the characteristics and behaviors of the management team. They were afraid and unwilling to risk. Risk caused ostracization from organizational advancement and created factors of leprosy if your decision was not valued by the executive team.

What the board of directors hoped to achieve in their movement to an administrative style was not working. In fact, the next election which occurred during this three year period saw four of the seven board members losing their seat. The major force in their demise was the employees who actively campaigned against their retention. Employees had made choices to fight back to regain what they had lost. Relationships were strained, unions fought against each other, departments fought against each other for budget dollars and positions, and managers withheld information to give themselves a better place in the organizational structure.

The executive team seemed oblivious to these actions, marching forward with their plan that was without a following. They just knew they were right, and if the employees did not understand, they would replace the decision making tier throughout the organization with "new blood"—outsiders who had no allegiance to the organizational history. The next fourteen major hires were "city management types" who would understand the directions of the executive team. Unfortunately, all of the new hires found themselves caught between the crossfire of the two perspectives. Four left within six months and eleven aligned themselves with the employees; new choices and new decisions had been made. There had become a misalignment of the direction of the board of directors to those of a chief executive officer and his team bent on a direction and a set of choices that disempowered staff, demoralized and devalued technical skills, and reduced potential for risking and embracing change.

Unsupported choices, ineffective decision making, and personal discounting had become the direction of the company. What once was an organization held to the highest esteem, filled with the highest skilled technical people perceived as a family of caring and directed staff, was now in a shamble. What is hard to fathom in the situation is the knowledge that this chief executive officer had been terminated from two previous organizations for creating the same set of shambles. What is even more disturbing and dysfunctional is the realization that the actions of Joseph occur on a daily basis in corporations throughout the United States and Europe and that it continues.

The issue of choice is critical in this example and is the topic of this book. Executives, managers, and employees are constantly confronted with making choices. The decisions we make consistently and continually impact the actions and outcomes of personal and organizational functioning. The first choice that was important in the actions of the chief executive officer was the decision to see the functioning of the organization and the employees as a problem. The concept of problems often initializes actions of codependence—fix it, blame others, start over, expunge the problem, the person, the system in place—that establish a chain reaction that is hard to overcome. The choice in the aforementioned situation was to disregard history, disregard organizational process, disregard organizational icons, and devalue the human condition of the firm. The choice of the chief executive officer was to create organizational psychosis. *Organizational psychosis* is the creation of a set of norms and actions that craft structures unable to distinguish the rational process of change and development from the irrational structures of power, control, disempowerment, and dysfunction. It is the development of dysfunction, based on a set of prescribed strategies that increase the potential for control through the devaluing and creation of personal mistrust and personal self-esteem, to create a dependence on the organizational leader and the organizational structure to validate one's need for belonging, and therefore perpetuation of the system that created the need for belonging beyond normal parameters of interdependence. Organizational psychosis is based on the content of thought, form of thought, perception, affect, sense of self, volition, impaired interpersonal functioning and relationship to the external world, and psychomotor behavior as it pertains to organizational development, organizational structure, and organizational change. To help you process the concepts of organizational psychosis, understanding of the varying components of the psychosis can be most helpful.

CONTENT OF THOUGHT

How one thinks is critical to the content of thought components of organizational psychosis. The thought processes are fragmented or compartmentalized with little understanding of the interrelationship between ideas and action. Thoughts perpetuate the implausible and senses of persecution, and paranoia perpetuates the belief that one is being spied upon or having false rumors spread about one's behavior, beliefs, or actions. The stronger the belief that persecution is occurring, the stronger the desire to create the same for others or to develop strategies to discredit and discount the value of the individual in the eyes of the organization and the organizational decision makers. Grandiosity and somatic and nihilistic delusions become the norm of the organization and its members.

FORM OF THOUGHT

The form of thought is the loosening of traditionally strong associations in which there is a constant shift between ideas in such a fashion that it is difficult to pinpoint a common thread within the organization other than the present dysfunction. Consistent statements that lack sincerity for meaningful relationships become the new norm. There is often a sparseness in speech, allowing only one person—usually the organizational leader—to state issues and factors without meaning and with little substance—"sounding" good, but creating stages of vagueness, abstract comments, or overly concrete and repetitive statements.

PERCEPTION

Perceptions are guided by fear factors that suggest survivability is based on the ability of the person or the system to assimilate the actions of the majority or the leaders. Usually both assimilation of the whole and the part are present. Some persons will embrace the control factors of the leaders, others will embrace the rebellion of the masses. In both cases, there is a denial and abdication of the self and the organizational system that has potential for positive development for the easier path of negative development.

AFFECT

Affect guides behavior. Psychotic affect is based on the noncongruence of one's behavior with the feelings that are pervasive within the organization. Where one experiences fear, personal affect is dysfunctional; when the behavior is jovial, the personal behavior appears trusting, amorous, and clinging. Where affect is flat, listless, lethargic, or protective, psychosis has set in the organization and the person. The person may complain that they no longer respond with normal emotional intensity. In fact, the person may often appear depressed, despondent, and listless on the job.

SENSE OF SELF

The ability to sense yourself as unique, capable, competent, and responsive has been replaced by a new belief that you are incompetent and unable to perform analytical and usual functions without direction. Self-direction is gone and you find yourself focused on what others believe is the direction for you. An example can be knowing that you are an excellent writer, but find yourself doubting your abilities because of the continual "wordsmithing" of your work by others to achieve a political end. You are told that you cannot write, and over time begin to believe that the statements are true.

VOLITION

There is a disturbance in self-initiation, goal directed activity, and role functioning. What used to be clear and easy is now unclear and extremely difficult. You find that interest is lost, drive is nonexistent, and the ability to follow a course of action to its logical conclusion has somehow escaped you. You feel consistently lost.

IMPAIRED INTERPERSONAL FUNCTIONING AND RELATIONSHIP TO THE EXTERNAL WORLD

Where development of relationships used to come easily, there has come a difficulty. This may take the form of social withdrawal and emotional detachment. The person may become significantly egocentric, focusing on self. They may become clinging to persons they know (or intrusive upon persons they do not know very well), and fail to recognize that excessive closeness makes some people uncomfortable. They may take out frustration and anger on persons close to them, constantly yelling and raising their voice without recognition of the change.

PSYCHOMOTOR BEHAVIOR

As all the other factors occur, increases in reactivity to the environment and in "sick-building" syndromes, as well as decreases in spontaneous activity, may occur. Where office gatherings use to occur on a regular basis, or where going out for a drink with the group after work was a

common occurrence, reductions in these activities begin with no explanation. People may appear catatonic in the organization, or rigid in
their behavior and actions. There may be an increase in odd mannerisms,
grimacing behavior, or fidgeting throughout the office environment.
These dysfunctional actions and thoughts have become all too common
in our organizations and communities, and too often the response from
our corporate leaders has perpetuated the dysfunctions rather than
deflate them.

THE LEADER'S RESPONSIBILITY

Organizational leaders are the official guides of organizational process,
health, wellness, sanity, congruence, and creations. It is difficult to recognize that critical role as a leader when the majority of actions are
based on compartmentalization. Leaders too often focus on the bottom
line, the new product line, the lack of a manager's agreement with a
given perspective, the reaction of a board member, the actions of a
union, or the survivability factor of maintaining a particular power perspective. In so doing, they assist in the destruction and demise of an
opportunity to lead and make significant change that can guide the
present and future.

   The leader in any organization is instilled with the obligation to
maintain the safety and well being of all the employees within that organization, as well as the product or service that the organization pro-
duces. When compartmentalization guides the actions and the
decision-making process, the leader participates in a tangent of choice.
Tangents of choice are those decisions we make that react to the moment,
the situation, the obvious, and the easiest. Tangents of choice impede
the potential to see the whole picture. They focus on the obvious or
easiest strategy for "fixing an issue of situation," and they perpetuate the
observation of the issue as a problem rather than an experience.

THE POLITIZING OF CHOICE AND
DECISION MAKING

As I thought of organizational psychosis, I was struck by a central theme
that often drives the psychotic reactions of a company. Organizational
politics are an insidious culprit in the process of choice. Consider this
recent example of a city in the state of Washington. Over an eighteen-
month period, the organization has struggled with the concept of diversity. The desired outcome of the management was to instill a level of
empowerment among the employees to frame their organizational destiny and simultaneously embrace the changes in the workforce and the

community. The employees took the management team at their word and developed focus groups to understand the issues. A consultant was called in to help the organization frame its process for decision making, hiring, promotion, business strategy, and community relations. As the staff continued over this period of time, relationships improved among the varying ethnic groups within the organization. There was an identification of the impediments to change and newness, and there were strategies developed by the employees to wade through the issues. Management was involved throughout the process.

In December 1994, the organization published a draft report of the findings of the diversity team internally to the organization. No mention was made at the time to the indictments and intervention strategies for white males and their need to change to embrace the present organization and the future. In March 1995, the fire chief, a member of the committee, began to feel uncomfortable with the agreements originally made, not because they were inaccurate but because the indictments impacted his political standing within the organization. He spoke with the chairperson of the committee, who shared that empowerment of the employees had a payoff that would move the organization to the next step of creating an inclusive organization—a high outcome of the process. The fire chief, uncomfortable with that answer, went to the city manager, suggesting that releasing the report in its present form would hurt them both politically. The city manager directed the chairperson of the committee to remove the "causes" of frustration and hurt from the report. No mention of the impact of a white male dominated system would be allowed or tolerated.

The employees on the committee felt betrayed. They had followed the rules and politics that were now guiding the final direction of the organization. Politics often craft a reality that is inconsistent with the views and beliefs of the employees of a system. To frame reality based on political intent often creates an unreal perspective that is only held by the leaders of a system. *Politics* are the carefully crafted strategies designed to frame a perspective, approach, or ideology, to hook the masses into following that view for the present and future. They set the stage for a choreographed picture and process that allows the leader to feel comfortable, irrespective of the beliefs and attitudes of the masses, and block the common thread discussed in the "form of thought" component of organizational psychosis. Politics create consistent statements that lack sincerity for meaningful relationships to form, and allow only the leader to state the issues and the factors, often without meaning. They are guided by fear, suggesting that survivability is based on the person or the system, to assimilate the actions of the fear of consequences created by truth or group belief as an issue of perception.

Politics guide affect and behavior—the noncongruent actions of the leader versus the feelings and behaviors present within the organization—and guide the sense of self, creating delusional beliefs about the uniqueness, competency, and responsiveness of a leader or a system to respond to the need for self-direction within an organization. Politics impact the volition of people and systems in framing goal-directed activity and role functioning, and make it hard to see the clarity in an issue or idea, because they can change the sense of clarity. When organizational leaders become political, interpersonal functioning and relationships become more difficult in the management of the work of the organization.

THE IMPACT OF POLITICS ON ORGANIZATIONAL PROCESS

Members of the Organizational Development Network, the American Society of Training and Development, the Employee Assistance Association, the American Psychological Association, and organizational and clinical psychologists constantly confront the impact of the political process on the individual and the system. In my own practice, I am constantly brought into organizations after the organizational leader experiences a crisis, or after the traditional business consultant has intervened with a strategy for improving organizational effectiveness and profit. Too often, politics and the lack of integrity and ethics guide the decision-making process of the leader and the consultant. Too often, no assessment of the impact of a strategy is considered *before* the actions of the leader or the consultant are taken. Consultants often say it was what I was contracted and directed to do; leaders often say the strategy met the need of the stockholders or personal grandisement. Rarely do I find the leader or consultant saying, "Let's assess the organizational *and* personal systems impacted by this or that strategy." Each time politics or control drive the strategy or the intervention, the process of organizational psychosis becomes more entrenched within the organization. The more the delusions expand, the more the strategies empower the delusions, and the person and the system become more dysfunctional and more lost.

It is intriguing to watch organizational leaders and consultants participate in the dysfunctional process. Clinically, it is termed *habit disorder*, and the essential features of this disorder are intentional and repetitive behaviors that are nonfunctional, serving no constructive or socially acceptable purpose. Sometimes habit disorders are brief and episodic, but more often they are chronic, and follow the leader from job to job, career to career, decision to decision, choice to choice. It can

be emotional or physical, but always creates a repetition that is noticeable to the employees underneath. The impact is the same—psychosis
becomes the norm of the organization.

A SHARING OF THE DYSFUNCTION

It is important to state that the organizational leader is not alone in
these issues. Boards of directors, members of the executive team, and
shareholders of a corporation all participate in the development of organizational psychosis. It is also important to state that no one but the
leaders and decision makers are accountable for the psychosis that is
occurring throughout American and European corporate structures. It
is not the only levels of dysfunction that have begun to occur; rather it
is the framework of dysfunction that is unfortunately guiding too much
of organizational life. In Chapters 3 and 4, we will see how the employee
level and each level of management has taken on a dysfunctional track
that permeates all of organizational decision making and choice.

ORGANIZATIONAL HISTORY AS THE BASELINE OF CHOICE

CHAPTER 3

Impacts on Managers and Leader Decision Making and the Makings of Manic-Depressives

In Chapter 2, we began to discuss the choices often made by executives to resolve, explore, or craft changes without a clear understanding of the impacts of their choices. In that framework, psychosis often becomes the norm in organizational existence. This chapter focuses on the history and style of the organization creating a manic depressive world and workplace for managers and leaders.

Think of your organization and your path to becoming a manager or leader. Think of the feelings you developed in moving through your organization or the different organizations where you have worked. Remember the executive or manager who was ruthless, uncaring, and cynical. Think also of the good experiences, and remember how each experience, positive or negative, began to shape some of your thinking, and an enormous amount of your behavior.

The process of thinking and remembering these experiences is "recalling your organizational history." Managers are often frustrated by their organizational history, yet continually experience privilege and payoff from their movement within organizations, irrespective of the trauma and damage created in the history-making process.

Joyce is the director of a Human Resources Department within an organization. She was hired because of her "history" of crafting reasonable change within organizations. She has been with the new organization eighteen months. At first, she was prompt to work, smiling with her employees, listening to their long-term concerns, and collaborating with them to create strategies that would alter the issues that were left unresolved for long periods of time. Within three months, her staff began to experience a noticeable change in her behavior. The first signs were absences from work. Joyce would come to work an hour and a half late, or she would call in sick and just not show up. The second sign was a change in her interactions with staff. She was increasingly short, flailing her arms in discussions, yelling at persons of color, discounting or shutting off communication from staff, and wringing her hands. The third sign was an increase in her weight. Joyce gained approximately thirty pounds in one year and seemed to gorge in the organizational cafeteria, as though she were trying to soothe her feelings and frustrations. The fourth sign was a disheveled appearance in her clothing.

Joyce spoke of feelings of hopelessness and pessimism and began to have chronic aches and pains—persistent bodily symptoms that were not caused by physical disease. She even found herself visiting a chiropractor on a weekly basis. Joyce was exhibiting signs of depression.

It might be easy to settle with this diagnosis of Joyce; however, there were other signs that suggested a different issue. The nature of the business of human resources often focuses on projects that are required to comply with emerging law or case law that impacts organizational action. This existed for Joyce in her role. She would show increased energy bursts, unrealistic beliefs about her technical knowledge and abilities, display aggressive reactions to frustrations, and experience racing and disconnected thoughts. Joyce would become excited and animated, almost in uncontrollable ways, as she focused on projects. Joyce's behavior of yelling, fast-paced action, focus on a singular point of view, unwillingness to hear other perspectives, seeing perspectives of other people as out to get her or destroy her work product, executives being unsympathetic to disruptions or changes in the work, and issues of time and explosions in front of staff all suggested that there was a manic, out-of-control component to Joyce's behavior.

It was not clear to the staff what was going on. Still, they felt confused, frustrated, angry, and unwilling to be supportive of her behavior. Joyce was in trouble on her job. Rather than seek some assistance, she made the choice to be strong and "tough it out," so that nothing would happen to her job. She looked around and saw that her behavior was not any different from other managers. They all felt stressed when projects were on board, and seemed somewhat hefty and out of shape. All talked of the workload and their frustration with the "manner in which work had to be accomplished on the job." In effect, Joyce perceived her behavior as normal and a part of the "organizational culture."

Joyce was correct. The culture of her organization and its organizational history bred manic-depressive managers. The experiences of Joyce are experiences of many managers within corporate and public organizations. There is a fragmented and compartmentalized approach to organizational action.

In a June 1995 report by Smith Kline Beecham Clinical Laboratories, depression and manic depression are considered the hidden diseases affecting 18 million people annually, most of whom never seek treatment. Depression affects the mind, body, and behavior. It robs victims of energy, pleasure, sleep, and confidence. An estimate of the impact of depression is an annual cost of $3,000 per employee to each employer. Eighty percent of depressed employees can be effectively treated, but only one-third of the affected persons ever seek treatment.

There are several depressive disorders. Major depression is characterized by persistent feelings of sadness, worthlessness, and emptiness that interfere with work, sleep, and daily activity. Dysthymia is a less severe form of chronic depression that impairs (but does not necessarily disable) normal functioning. Manic-depressive illness, or bipolar depression, involves alternating cycles of depression and elation. The incidence of depression is highest among people during their prime working years, between twenty-five and fifty-four. Women are twice as likely as men to suffer from major depression and dysthymia, as shown in Figure 3.1.

Figure 3.2 depicts the extent of mental disorders in 1990 among adults. You can see by the chart that 2 million persons were impacted by schizophrenia, 17.5 million by depressive disorders, 2.2 million by manic-depressive illness, 9.2 million by major depression, 9.9 million by dysthymia, and 23.2 million by anxiety disorders. There is a real connection between the emotional health of our workforce and society, and the strategies employed within workplaces. Our executives, managers, and boards of directors are not effectively identifying or addressing the issues of health and wellness of people, and it is costing American corporations billions of dollars.

Our corporate structures have compartmentalized, fragmented, and detached human factors from organizational decisions and, in so doing, have allowed the bottom line to craft poor decisions that are costly in the long-term forecast of business and personal health. Consider these facts from two recent studies. Economists from the Analysis Group, Inc., and the Massachusetts Institute of Technology estimated the total cost of depression and mood disorders in 1990 at $43.7 billion annually, far higher than previous estimates. The findings were based on treatment costs, as well as lost productivity and wages, due to the three leading types of depressive disorders: manic depression, major

Figure 3.1
Lifetime Prevalence of Affective Disorder

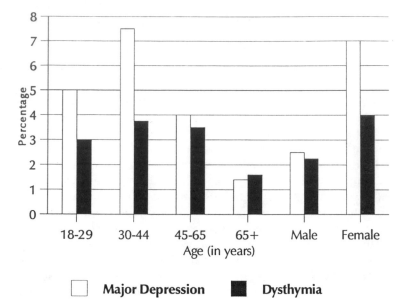

Source: Lee N. Robbins and Darrel A. Regier, eds. *Psychiatric Disorders in America.* Philadelphia: The Free Press, 1994. Reprinted with permission.

Figure 3.2
Number of U.S. Adults (in Millions) with Mental Disorders, 1990

Schizophrenia	**2.0**
Depressive Disorders	**17.5**
Manic-depressive illness	2.2
Major depression	9.2
Dysthymia	9.9
Anxiety disorders	**23.2**
Phobia	20.1
Panic disorder	2.4
Obsessive-compulsive disorder	3.9
Antisocial personality disorder	**2.8**
Severe cognitive impairment	**5.0**

Source: National Institute of Mental Health.
Note: Some people have more than one mental disorder. Therefore, the sum of all disorders is greater than the total.

depression, and dysthymia. The study broke out direct and indirect costs of depression with $12.4 billion in direct medical expenses, $7.5 billion in lost wages due to suicides, and $23.8 billion in lost productivity (consisting of $11.7 billion in excessive absenteeism and $12.1 billion in lower productivity). First Chicago Corporation studied its mental health costs from 1988 through 1992 and found that depression was its costliest medical condition, accounting for 52 percent of the mental health costs of its 18,000 employees. It caused an average of forty short-term disability days lost, compared to an average of twenty-nine days for non–mental health disabilities.

The message is evident; we are paying too little attention to the emotional health of our organizations, and in so doing, are creating an ill workforce. Some may say that the health of these persons is their own doing and not caused by the workplace. In fact, terminations of employees after worker compensation suits suggest that the employees came to work with these issues and the organization is just weeding out the problem areas.

We must therefore revisit Chapter 1, where discussion of the choices becomes an important and critical discussion for us in assessing organizational history and its impact on the growth and movement of managers and leaders. In the dynamics of choice, we spoke of the antagonistic process of our leaders. Remember, antagonism perpetuates the blaming process and defeats the potential for the inclusion and participation of people in the decision-making process. The dissonance of choice speaks to what is out of whack or perceived differently by different people about the same issue. When these managers delude themselves into believing that there is nothing wrong—that weight gain, loss of perspective, loss of energy, feelings of guilt and worthlessness, and chronic aches are just a part of "growing older"—the dissonance is strong and the choices are increasingly poorer and more costly to the organization. When managers continue to make decisions on little information, the tangents of choice become critical in the development of patterns within the decision-making process. Finally, as these choices, that ultimately create another problem, are made from one project or situation to another, the incidents of choice are prevalent. Our choices around our organizational history can breed success and wellness, or they can perpetuate illness and costly consequences.

Initial discussions with Joyce by the organizational psychologist on staff focused on the noticeable changes. The approach suggested by the psychologist was a "fix-it" approach to reduce the overall cost to the organization. He focused on the obvious, and compartmentalized the treatment to fix the person—yet no discussion ensued about the illness of the organization. The insidious nature of organizational disconnects is extreme. Rarely does an organization focus on the long view, ensuring that all the connections are complete. Where organizations work

diligently to connect the fiscal pieces of the pie, little attention is given
to the human pieces. The constant choices of the organization perpetuate the production and health care costs that continue to skyrocket in
the 1990s.

What are we describing in this chapter? In Chapter 2, I described
organizational psychosis and its impact on the organization. Here I am
talking about organizational depression. *Organizational depression* is the
creation of a set of norms that cause a disturbance of mood, accompa-
nied by a full range of disconnecting activities that block the orderly
and smooth interaction of the system, with the people accountable for
developing rational outcomes to accomplish organizational business.
Mood refers to a prolonged emotion that colors the whole psychic life
and generally involves depression or elation. Sometimes, the organizational behavior is melancholic or chronic. Effectually, the mood disturbance is sufficient to alter the occupational and interpersonal
functioning of the organization and its individuals with one another.
Associated issues can be levels of grandiosity or imperviousness. In the
bipolar phases, swings in mood will, at times, appear euphoric, unusu-
ally cheerful or high, uncritical self-confidence, or belief that organizational actions or changes can occur in spite of clear information that
suggests that continuation on the existing change path will create significant difficulties.

Frequently, there are flights of ideas changing from one topic or organizational function to another with no closure on the activities. The
most prevalent depressive content is the excessive planning, participation, or extreme caution to "select" the right option or decision, resulting in "no decision or option"—thereby maintaining ineffective and
incomplete results. Often, the manager is unaware of the intrusive,
domineering, or demanding nature of the requests or action occurring.
In the manic phase, expansiveness, unwarranted optimism, grandiosity,
and lack of judgment are the key behaviors. Organizationally, decisions
that continue on a poor path are examples of this behavior.

Consider an executive who is asked to obtain feedback from the employees to assess the efficacy of programs and policies that have been implemented. The feedback returns, and it strongly states that the policies
and programs have been ineffective. In reporting the results to the
board of directors, the manager "paints the results" in a light that does not
resemble what employees stated. The employees experience the depressive
side of the executive's actions; the executive experiences the melancholic
and euphoric side of his actions. The organization and all the employees
lose in the choice made by the executive. The depressive episodes become stronger. Employees find themselves unable to sit still, pace the
floor or the room, wring their hands, and pull on their hair, skin, and
clothing. Increases in slowed responses to executive statements become

evident and a decrease in energy occurs. The organizational depression is upon us. Unrealistic evaluations of self occur, coupled with feelings of worthlessness and inadequacy. Difficulties in concentration and constant reproach become the new norm.

Employees may find themselves tearful without incident, brooding, or excessive in ruminating about issues or actions within the organization. Diminished interest in the work occurs and absences and health conditions begin to occur. The organizational depression has taken hold, and the need for fiscal resources to continue with life presses upon the employee the hopelessness of the situation. The hopelessness breeds fatigue and a loss of energy, with a diminished ability to think and act decisively.

THE IMPACT OF ORGANIZATIONAL HISTORY ON MANAGER DECISION MAKING

As I thought of the issues of organizational depression and their impact on personal and organizational action, I was immediately struck by the extent to which lifelong organizational patterns perpetuate the delusion that normalcy is occurring within the organization. Every time an organization determines a process or procedure for how something is to occur, the organization is building history. If the process is political, and promotion and upward mobility are based on that political process, history is in the making. Every time a manager makes a decision to choose a course of action that perpetuates itself without consideration to its impact on others, organizational history is made. Every time an officer of a company says, "I don't like this about that employee, find a way to get rid of him," and the manager follows that decision, organizational history is made. Every time a codification of the inappropriate or political decision is made, organizational history is created. When that decision-making process is compartmentalized to the particular situation, is fragmented and different from the pattern of decisions that have been made previously, or discounts all the information for only select information that supports a given decision, then the organization has made choices. Dynamics of choice, dissonance of choice, tangents of choice, and incidents of choice have occurred that impact the holistic potential of the organization.

THE LOSS OF ORGANIZATIONAL SPIRIT

The development of a depressive organization occurs when there is no clear direction or vision for the organization. Managers represent the binding glue between the values and vision of an organization, the organization's spirit, and the rest of the workforce. Managers are the keepers of the vessel of the spirit. When the spirit is challenged, broken, or is in the background of the organization, superimposed by disjointed action, the organization begins to take on a depressive and dysfunctional character. This character is one of poor mental health.

One must continually ask, "What does it take to repair and make whole this organization?" This is the challenge of organizational history. The histories of organizations that I am describing are wrought with pain, trauma, compartmentalization, and fragmented action. Too often, organizational history is taken for granted as being without real form or thought. Nothing could be further from the truth.

Organizational history and spirit are intricately connected as the yin and yang of the organizational life. How the two work in tandem often dictates the extent to which the organization remains healthy, and how the managers remain healthy (versus becoming depressed and dysfunctional).

Every organization has an ethos that frames its way of interfacing with the world. This ethos sets the tone for how the organization provides service to the community and its customers, views and values its employees, frames its policies and processes, and how the organization values the "humanity" of its employees. The humanity value becomes a critical spiritual and spirit-oriented process. When organizations are inattentive to this spirit, it wanes and the humanity is lost.

Look at the following example of an organization and its leaders. A major utility corporation has wanted to transform its perspective from an engineering model to a modified public administration model. This change was created by the advent of a new board of directors in 1990. The new board was environmentally proactive, wanting to ensure that critical ecosystems were maintained. In their zeal to achieve their outcomes, they selected a general manager who would be subservient to their will, subjugating employees and managers to a process of change that was not always clear and direct. During a four-year period, managers were told that they were wrong and not valued and were dehumanized and discounted by the board of directors. The general manager continually slashed critical resources that would have allowed managers to be successful in their roles. Projects were fast and furious. Day-to-day work increased, and the resources and technologies required to help them be successful were not forthcoming. The board of directors continually stated that managers were inept, cutting their raises and perks. The board of directors elevated the unions to a position of equal, if not greater, authority to the managers, and watched an unhealthy battle occur. The general manager participated in the demise of the organization and its managers, seeing more and more depression and bipolar dysfunction grow within the organization. Four years later, the general manager was terminated and a new board of directors was installed into the organization. The cost was fear, mistrust, frustration, intense and constant tension, loss of energy, trepidation, and inaction. Managers believed that the spirit—what brought them to the organization—was gone, and they formed a management union.

This example is playing itself out throughout the United States. Depressive environments are created because organizational leaders have thrown away the organizational history and spirit for immediate short-term gains or a singularly focused direction. Depressive leaders emerge because of historical change. How we become leaders is often wrought with political and personal agendas rather than strategies that enhance the effectiveness and the vision of the organization. Abdicating knowledge of the history and spirit begins a concatenating process of destruction of people and systems that is hard to reverse. The spirit and history of the organization have been anastomatized and the resulting outcome is the creation of dysfunctional systems and people that are costly in image to the community and company, to the stockholders and public in health care costs and productivity losses, to the managers and employees in the denigration of the self and team, and to the extended families in the loss of the balance within the person's yin and yang.

This process of disregarding the yin and yang—the process of disregarding the humanity of the organization and its members—becomes a critical challenge of organizational leaders. Remembering the history, and determining its importance in furthering the value of the organization, becomes a central theme in the issue of choice. Remembering that choice is the pivotal and ultimate point in allowing people and systems to effectively move through the maze of rules, regulations, politics, and changes becomes an ever-present requirement to effectively maintain best business practices and best organizational health. The change in the process of choice by the board of directors and the general manager in the last example demanded that the values of the board and general manager were more important than the whole. Their choice began with the premise that the organization needed changing, in spite of evidence that it might have been functioning effectively. Their perspective began with the premise that the managers were wrong and bad, and all actions focused on proving that premise to the demise of the managers. When the process of change is selective and discounts all the factors in critical choices, fragmentation, detachment, and compartmentalization are again the outcomes that bind the new history of the organization. The selective process binds the organizational spirit so that it can no longer guide organizational action, and the best practices that were intended are lost.

The managers, like the executives, are trapped in a system of dysfunction, and the organization and its community of customers are the losers. However, it is important to understand that the employees also begin to embrace dysfunctional clinical traits that impact the business issues.

HOMOGENEITY OR DIVERSITY AS A BASELINE OF CHOICE

CHAPTER

4

Impacts on Employee and Customer Decision Making and the Makings of Neurotic Behavior

In Chapters 2 and 3, I described the issues of dysfunction that occur among executives and managers. In each chapter, I explicitly described the dysfunctions in clinical terms to import the seriousness of the issues, as well as to simultaneously address the underpinning that organizational leaders must recognize that a component of best business practices and business decision making is the recognition of the humanness and value sets of the organization and its members. This chapter focuses on the largest group of organizational life—the employees and the customers. Critical in this assessment is a recognition that all parties of an organization contribute to its wellness or its illness. Best business practices are not limited to the management of an organization, but rather, all persons impacted by the business are accountable for the development of practices that allow all to succeed and impact the product and service of the organization.

Mark is an African-American maintenance worker in a city government in Arizona. Mark has been frustrated over the past six years with his managers in the organization. He believes that the managers maintain a double standard regarding allowable work standards. Often he senses that he is scrutinized more comprehensively than his white counterparts. As time has passed, Mark has raised the issue of perceived racism to the managememt team and the affirmative action officer. To his sadness, Mark has seen nothing positive come out of his risk-taking behavior.

Over time, Mark has met with a number of employees who are non-white. They each present similar pictures of the organizational management process and the knowledge that others feel the same way, which has bolstered Mark's vehemence toward the perceived uneven treatment. Mark has become more vocal in early morning muster meetings, openly challenging the management for their lack of fairness and equitable treatment.

Management within the organization feels that Mark is crying wolf. They do not believe that any racism exists within the organization and feel that Mark received his job based on being an affirmative action hire. They just sense that they are assisting Mark with the development of his skills. They are tired of being accused of racial discrimination and unfair treatment and have become hardened to Mark's words.

Mark and the management are at odds with one another and the situation has grown to total mistrust, anger, disregard, and discount of anything either group has to say. An impasse has been reached.

Adrienne is a female first-line supervisor in a computer corporation in northern California. Adrienne is very proud of her accomplishments. She has achieved a Ph.D. in computer science with a specialty in robotics. She was recently hired by a major computer corporation as a project manager of a critical robotics project. Reporting to her in this role are six Asian males and four East Indian males, all with credentials equal to hers.

Adrienne has not found the immersion into supervision to be a rewarding experience. She is the first female project manager and finds that the staff reporting to her discounts her direction and leadership. She senses that she would not be experiencing these issues if her gender was male. She is frustrated and has begun to become hardened, very direct, pointed in her communication, unfeeling, and suspicious of the actions of her employees. She finds herself writing up the employees for everything that is not correct or as she directed. The staff pulls away from her and begins to leave out critical information regarding the project.

Management above Adrienne has become increasingly concerned with the progress of the project and Adrienne's leadership. Time is of the essence and the project must get back on track. She is called into a meeting by the management team, and they express their concerns. Adrienne feels trapped to respond and shows that she is having a difficult time managing the work and leading the staff. She gives platitudes to the issues in an attempt to deflect the issues as she sees them. Management terminates her employment and Adrienne leaves feeling set up and discounted. She reports that the organization was sexist and that the corporate world does not do anything to help women be successful. She has a jaundiced view of corporate America.

George is the head of a union within a union environment. He has worked for the organization for fifteen years, and has been heavily involved in the development of the union from infancy to its current adult status. He has worked diligently to achieve the best for its members, trying to balance the union's position with the needs of the corporate structure, and to change the present to a new future.

George's membership is untrusting and wary of any overtures from him or any other management and the board of directors. Any alteration must be met with additional compensation for the members if there is to be any change. The union meetings appear similar to a brawl—angry shouting, castigations of anyone who wants to work with management to create a different reality, and loud protests to any "consorting with the enemy." Over the past four years, the union has made many strides within the organization to advance their perspective. This approach has been a blend of adversarial and collaborative processes that has created more distance between management and the union.

George has become increasingly uncomfortable with the behavior of his union. They pride themselves on their noncollaboration with management, and deride him every time he collaborates to make a change. They have forced him to experience more and more stress and weight gain. He finds their behavior, personally and as a union, oppositional and contrary. George is frustrated.

George has decided to not run for another term as president of the union. In fact, he finds the behaviors of management and the union to be so dysfunctional that he is retiring from the organization.

A group of ethnically diverse employees are filing a lawsuit against their organization. They find that the organization callously discriminates against persons of color and rationalizes their behavior to justify their actions. Over the past four years, a new chief executive officer has terminated or demoted every person of color in the management ranks and has placed nonminorities in the roles. The ethnically diverse employees state that one or two could have been nonperformers, but ten nonperformers is unrealistic, and the organization must be opposed in their actions.

These scenes are played out throughout the United States in corporations and governments every day. Paulo Freire, a noted sociologist, wrote in his book, *Pedagogy of the Oppressed,*

Dehumanization, which marks not only those whose humanity has been stolen, but also those who have stolen it, is a distortion of the vocation of becoming more fully human. This distortion occurs within history. The struggle for humanization, for the emancipation of labor, for the overcoming of alienation, for the affirmation of men and women as persons would be meaningless. This struggle is possible only because humanization, although a concrete historical fact, is not a given destiny but the result of an unjust order that engenders violence in the oppressors, which in turn dehumanizes the oppressed. This then is the great humanistic and historical task of the oppressed: to liberate themselves and their oppressors.

The issues present in each of the described situations speak to the lack of inclusion and participation of organizations and their leaders to ensure the success and health of the organizations. That the inclusion of diversity and quest for authenticity creates an awareness and an opportunity for people to partner with the organization in crafting a better present and future that binds the values and beliefs of the organization somehow gets lost. In that loss, the organization and the person experience a dysfunction that is affective in nature.

CONDUCT DISORDERS AND OPPOSITIONAL DISORDERS

The actions of an organization structurally, procedurally, and psychodynamically can significantly alter the developmental actions of the employees within the organization. The situations heretofore mentioned often lead to two clinically dysfunctional processes—conduct and oppositionally defiant disorders. They are developmental disorders because they occur over time. In the clinical setting, they occur in infancy and adolescence. Often organizationally, they occur when there is lack of clarity regarding the rules and structure, when the psychodynamic process of the organization is focused on control and power, or when the change process within the organization is focused on noninclusive strategies that allow a few to make decisions that impact the whole. These are chronic disorders that impact adaptive functioning, etiologic factors, familial patterns, reciprocal social interactions, communication, imaginative activity, and acts of antisocial behavior.

Conduct disorders are a persistent pattern of conduct in which the basic rights of others, as well as major societal and organizational norms, are violated. The behavioral pattern is typically present in the workplace among peers and superiors. Physical aggression may become commonplace, and increased acts of stealing within the organization will be noticed. These are mostly covert acts termed "borrowing" by the employee. You will usually find increased utilization of tobacco, liquor, and recreational drugs. Concern for how others feel will decrease, and setting up others to fail will become a commonplace occurrence. Self-esteem is usually low, though the person may begin to project multiple images of being tough. This was especially evident in the example of Mark, the African-American employee.

Oppositional defiant disorders have as an essential pattern a negativistic, hostile, and defiant behavior, without the more serious violations of the basic rights of others that are prevalent in conduct disorders. These persons will be argumentative, frequently losing their temper. Cursing and angry outbursts are especially aimed toward persons in authority. You will also find them easily annoyed, and they may take their frustrations out on safe individuals who they consider their friends. They will blame others for their own mistakes and difficulties, and will usually deny their involvement in any of the dysfunctional actions occurring. They actively defy the rules, and work toward changing them to their advantage. These persons, like those with conduct disorders, have low self-esteem, mood lability, low frustration tolerance, and temper outbursts. There may be some increase in the use of psychoactive drugs and alcohol out of the self-medicating of the frustration. The more the person believes that the organization is "out to subjugate them," the more likely oppositional or conduct dysfunction will occur.

Employees feel trapped by the processes of the organization and search for strategies to defeat or change the processes as a form of protection. In my second book, *Organizational Violence: Creating a Prescription for Change*, I wrote about the incongruous competition that is created when employees experience a "violent" organizational structure. In it I stated that "the incongruence is the inability of the person or system to effectively find a balance between building people and building systems toward an outcome that fosters creativity and wholeness. Instead, the concept of competition pits one against another, with the outcome of defeat of the other as the primary goal. . . . We suggest becoming collaborative in our approach to developing work and people, yet we create competitive strategies for beating our business competitors to the delivery of a product." Too often, each approach we select furthers the conduct and oppositional dysfunction, making it impossible to break a cycle that belies all rational interactions between employees and managers, and between organization and community.

Let us look again at the components of the conduct and oppositional process that bind our hands and impact our decision making for the present and the future.

ADAPTIVE FUNCTIONING

Adaptive functioning refers to the person's effectiveness in areas of social skill development, communication development and daily living, or vocational functioning, and how well the person meets the standards of personal independence and social responsibility expected in the role that they perform. Adaptive functioning is often influenced by motivation and emotional, vocational, or social opportunities. In the context of organizations, the degree to which employees sense the opportunity for inclusion, participation, evaluation, and development of their skills and abilities to move effectively through the organization, impacts their sense of adaptive functioning. Where employees do not sense opportunities abounding, a chronic dysfunction will begin to develop personally that is directly tied to the experiences within the organization.

Behavioral symptoms in the adaptive dysfunction can include passivity, dependency, low self-esteem, low frustration tolerance, aggressiveness, poor impulse control, and self-injurious or destructive behaviors. These behaviors may be learned or they can be conditioned behaviors based on environmental and organizational factors.

ETIOLOGICAL FACTORS AND FAMILIAL PATTERNS

Etiological factors are predominantly biological and psychosocial. Some of the issues are inborn errors. Where organizations historically are exclusive in the design and development of futures, they are biological in their approach to dysfunction within the employees and the organization's life. Where growth occurs etiologically in birthing, organizations will experience a deformed child, because the basis for the matrimonial union was ill conceived and ill planned. Where physical disorders of infections and traumas occur, organizations will experience infected work units and traumatized employees and managers. Where environmental influences abound for a person depriving a person of effective nurturing, organizations will engender the same dynamics in employees as the environmental factors distance and detach the critical nurturing needs of the organizational employees. The actions of the organization effectually destroy the life of the organization.

RECIPROCAL SOCIAL INTERACTION

The more employees experience a distancing within the organization, the more difficult it will be to develop significant interpersonal relationships. Issues of fear, mistrust, and protection will surpass any potential for risking. This impairment is predicated by the lack of responsiveness to interest in people. We often find managers and employees developing this distancing component. Social indifference, lack of personal or organizational intimacy, inability to cooperate and collaborate, and the union's perspective feed the dysfunction, and the attachment components are lost.

COMMUNICATION AND IMAGINATIVE ACTIVITY

Communication is prevalent in every mental dysfunction and business interaction. In the case of mental dysfunction and its application to business-related concerns, language and comprehension are the key factors. Organizationally, when leaders and boards have been unclear about the vision or outcomes of the organization, interpretations of communication become a significant problem for all impacted. This is especially true for employees within the organization. Jokes, puns, special situations, or special symbols within the organization will be misunderstood, lending rise to hostilities and problems within the organization. Impairments in imagination and creativity will become evident because energy is more focused on protection or revenge by the employee.

ANTISOCIAL BEHAVIOR

When all the other factors are present, antisocial behavior is the result of chronic dysfunction in each of the other previously discussed areas. Antisocial behavior is the culmination that displays the impairment in its most visible forms. Opposition to authority, disobedience, violation of the basic rights of others, inappropriate age-related behaviors, and violation of rules and regulations become the new norms of behavior.

BUSINESS CONCERNS

Willis Harman, a world renowned anthropologist, recently said at the World Business Academy meeting in San Francisco, "Business has become in this last half century the most powerful institution on the planet. The dominant institution in any society needs to take responsibility for the whole. This is a new role for business, not yet well understood and accepted."

As you think of your role to the community, managers, and employees, it becomes important to recognize the new role—the new requirement to embrace a holistic approach to business that marries fiscal and technical responsibility with the human quality—not as an afterthought, or as a tool for implementation of the varying product concerns, but as a vibrant and engaging partner to organizational and personal success. Best business practices embody the concept of people, systems, and the whole in realistic partnerships that define and frame the world and the interactions that govern. Business fosters economic and cultural interdependence and has helped to create the awareness of one's humanity, on one planet, sharing a common fate. Business holds the key to the transformational process and decisions that make life work for everyone.

HOMOGENEITY AND DIVERSITY

What becomes important as a driver in this process is assessing diversity and homogeneity. The issue of homogeneity is always raised by the disenfranchised or discounted employee or manager. The issue suggests that the "White Male Club" or "White Privilege" seeks a mirror image in the selection of leaders so that likeminded views will be achieved. As a simplistic perspective, this may be true; however, it is no different than Congress's current conservative agenda or accusations toward the other side about a diverse agenda. What is significant is determining the extent to which diversity and differing views, strategies, and thoughts are considered in the choices that are made within organizations. Suffice it to say, it appears that diversity loses for the sake of groupthink. How we make choices, what we consider in the choices, and what we project as the impact of the choices are essential and central to the issue of transforming decisions, and therefore lives, in the business and personal environment. The challenge for business is recognizing the enormous advantage in intercultural pathing (which we shall discuss in more detail later), and searching for strategies to utilize that intercultural path to effectively self-adopt new strategies that value and appreciate diversity.

The belief that because everyone is of the same ethnicity they believe and act the same is a real misnomer. Examples would be Jesse Jackson versus Clarence Thomas, Phil Graham versus Al Gore, the head of the Red Brigade versus the head of the Palestine Liberation Army. Diversity is the only true catalyst, as homogeneity is in itself a misnomer where people are involved. Business must recognize and accept that diversity exists, and that homogeneity is a product of politics and organizational history, not people.

Getting to the whole among business and people requires a re-examination of our history, spirit, and choices that frame cultural and economic interdependence. Tangents, incidents, and dynamics of choice all are components of making decisions that empower and embrace diversity, politics, and leadership.

Chapters 1 to 4 have focused on the situations that suggest that a transformation in business is required. They strongly suggest that the mental health of business is in severe trouble because we have avoided embracing the "business whole" that is required for successful organization movement and existence. Chapter 1 focused on organizational makeovers, suggesting that change is needed and paramount. The challenge is recognizing our participation in the discount of holism as a critical factor in the assessment and analysis process of business decision making. We have made poor decisions because we have rarely addressed all the factors essential to decisions that matter. The rest of this book helps us understand the impacts of that process, and what we can begin to do differently to transform what we are to what we can become.

MINI-EPILOGUE

An Assessment of the Current Business Environment: Issues for Consideration in Transforming Businesses

The first part of this book focuses on the dysfunctions that occur when businesses are intentional about profit and streamlining for the future without consideration of the full range of factors that impact effective choices. Businesses are in crisis. Crisis is defined as the nexus point which determines future decisions that guide action. Businesses are facing that nexus in 1995 and 1996. As a business professor and an organizational development and change consultant, I have watched businesses embrace fiscal constraint, streamlined structures, advanced technologies, increased need for greater skills, and more accountability to citizens and customers. What has not been embraced is the life of the organization—the spirit and blood of the organization. These are the values and the people within the organization that guide and maintain the long-term view of what the organization hopes to embody in the community and the economic world.

There has been a serious disconnect in the business world. There is a dysfunctional assumption that people will adjust to any and all changes that are purported by management or boards of directors. Nothing is further from the truth, as boards and management want the adaptations to follow a path of congruent action. To achieve that outcome, the human factor—the emotional health of organizational and personal actions—must be an equal factor in the decision-making process. Transforming business requires an inclusion of all the issues that impact the business.

Examples in the past ten years of organizational violence, destroyed communities, broken families, ill-fated merged corporations, murderous rages from discharged employees (irrespective of reasons), and increased charges of unfair treatment and racism suggest that corporations make bad choices. Not that the "heart" of the decision was inappropriate, rather that the "heart and head" surrounding the decision were not connected. Every time a business decision is made, and fiscal management is the only concern, the organizational mental health is threatened. Every time a decision is compartmentalized, fragmented, or detached, the opportunity for psychosis, depression, or conduct dysfunction is probable. Every time a decision impacting others excludes the impacted parties, frustrations, angers, hurt, and possible sabotage are probable.

Executives and boards should consider that 84 percent of the workforce spends 70 percent of the time getting their needs met through the work environment. Work is not just a place to earn a living; it often plays out Maslow's "hierarchy of needs." Work is a living experience, not an inanimate or abstract decision-making process. The values executives bring to work impact the employees who report to that director.

Recently, a student in the Masters of Arts in Business program at the California Institute of Integral Studies postulated that if business is a metaphor for living in the twenty-first century and beyond, then the concept of "living in business" must reflect the issues that impact sustainability for people and systems. The theorem of the student exactly impacts the strain of this book. Responsible business action and responsible decision making require decisions that sustain life for the people within the business and the people impacted by the business. This requires a thoughtful and thorough process of choosing that encompasses all the factors—fiscal, political, environmental, value laden, spiritual, and emotive—that are a part of business. Whether the business is a copy center, antique store, or a nonprofit, government, or major corporation; whether the business is a family oriented, two-person operation or a conglomerate like Bechtel Corporation; the factors are the same. Living is the prospective opportunity and sustainable transformation of the business process to be truly inclusive and profitable is the desired outcome.

Emotional holism, a balanced ego, and a sustained inclusion of employees' life experiences are parts of every decision that is made. Choosing to avoid the tangents, incidents, and dynamics of choice is essential to the creation of a healthy organizational environment. Strategic visioning and management processes of the recent past consider the makeup of the community, focusing on the changes that are required for transforming a city, corporation, or government. Environmental scanning, environmental impact reports, and social ecological strategies all require an inclusion of the emotive as a part of the sustainable decision. Business can do no less if it is to be sustainable in the present and future.

Therefore, think of the experiences that your managers, boards, stockholders, employees, and customers need to be complete in their decisions. Consider the impact of compartmentalization and fragmentation on the long-term health of the business. Assess the life force of the business, and recognize that a part of the life force is the well being of the employees. Look at the confrontations between unions and management since the air traffic controllers strike of 1982 and assess the degree to which management needs the unions to be successful; and consider whether the decisions made within corporations in the past five years have sustained the business in a healthy manner. If the decision you reach is yes, then your company has been focused on sustainability. If the decision reached is that issues continued to crop up around compensation, benefits, absences, productivity, product development, marketing, and sales, then it suggests that the choices made were ineffective because all the factors for a living business were not included.

This first section only addresses the situations that develop in organizations. Psychological development is an equal partner with economic development in the decision-making process of organizations. Without its consideration and active participation, psychotic and depressive processes unknowingly occur. Rules, regulations, procedures, strategies, visions, missions, gap assessments, environmental scans, strategic business modeling, functional outcome assessments, congruence matching, and modeling all require the inclusion of emotive assessment.

I am reminded of a sociologist speaking of the common man. Paulo Freire stated that where there is power, there is oppression. Businesses have always focused on control of the market, research, sales, rules, and people. Unfortunately, the issue of control has gotten out of hand. People and systems have been dissected, compartmentalized, fragmented, detached, and dehumanized to an extent that creates inhumane actions. On July 29, 1995, the American Psychoanalytic Association met in San Francisco. In the *San Francisco Chronicle*, it was reported that the psychoanalysts feared that businesses and people have merged into one entity. That entity, irrespective of race, is caught in the throes of poor development, bad choices, and misplaced values with a result of pathological behaviors that defeat the potential of the human being. Envy, greed, lust, hatred, abuse, avarice, discount, control, and dishonesty are the values and actions of modern society. The state of business as a metaphor for living is at risk.

Therefore, businesses need to reframe their actions and their choices if they are to survive the current state of affairs. Witness this statement by Freire:

Money is the measure of all things and profit the primary goal. For the oppressors, what is worthwhile is to have more, always more, at the cost of the oppressed having less or having nothing. As beneficiaries of a situation of oppression, the oppressors cannot perceive that if having is a condition of being, it is a necessary condition for all men. This is why their generosity is false. To the oppressor, humanity is a thing and they possess it as an exclusive right, as inherited property.

Over time, the oppressed gravitate to the behavior of the oppressor as an irresistible attraction, for being one of the haves is important. Self depreciation is another characteristic of the oppressed, which derives from their internalization of the opinion the oppressors hold of them. So often do they hear that they are good for nothing, that they cannot think, that they cannot write, that they know nothing, that they are unproductive, that they are lazy. They are peasants and feel inferior to the boss because the boss seems to be the only one who knows things and is able to run things.

The peasant is a dependent. He can't say what he wants. Before he discovers his dependence, he suffers. He let's off steam at work, at home, where he shouts at his friends, his co-workers, his spouse. He beats them, yells at them and is in despair. He complains, but doesn't let off steam at the boss because he thinks the boss is a superior being and he is afraid.

Business development and education have forgotten the feeling business entrepreneurs experienced in the creation of a new venture. The rush of feelings, the synergy in the stomach, the peace in the heart, the balanced calmness, and the thoughtful strategy were all connected as factors in recognizing that the business decision, the choice to create a business, was right. Somehow, focus on economic development and redevelopment has displaced the "feel" of the decision.

The emotional inclusion of people rehumanizes the human condition. For too long, business has created psychological dysfunction through its compartmentalization and fragmentation. To achieve its place in society as a living business, it must rethink its current strategies. We have only spoken of the situations, the dynamics that begin to occur because of business action and decision making. Each of us must consider the intent and desired outcome of our choices, and map the impact of the decision should our choice become reality. Managers, executives, boards of directors, and employees have enormous responsibility and accountability to one another. When we abdicate that responsibility, we perpetuate the dysfunctions that create insanity and trauma.

As you will see in continuing parts of this book, reframing one's business decision-making process, transforming business decision-making strategies, and embracing the emotional as an equal partner can transform work and enhance profits through the reduction of business costs.

PART II

PERSONAL HOOKS THAT IMPACT ORGANIZATIONAL EFFECTIVENESS

THE TRAPS THAT TEAR US APART

CHAPTER

5

How We Fail in Our Decision Making and Create Organizational and Personal Shame

Leland is a city manager in a southwestern city. He came to the city from a background of military service where he was accustomed to people doing exactly what he said. This style of personal and organizational control seemed to work well in his history, and he saw no reason why it should not work well for him in this new role as city manager. He immediately began to make changes within the organization—demanding briefings for all presentations to the city council, creating a war room for the analysis and decision-making process on critical projects, and changing leadership within the organization to persons who saw the world the way he did.

Leland had a no-nonsense manner and saw nothing wrong with "putting people in their place," or "barking orders." His favorite saying was, "If you don't like my methods, don't let the door hit you on the way out!" Leland had begun to create an environment of fear within the organization. It must have been working, because the city council routinely took only fifteen minutes to provide his annual performance evaluation with an outstanding rating.

Managers began to look for avenues of escape, with depression being a primary side effect of Leland's behavior. Over time, the managers felt trapped, stating that their manhood has been lost. "I feel so ashamed when I am around him. He castigates me in front of my employees. Everybody is on edge and I feel like the organization has become an evil place to work. They [the council] must like it because there has been no change in two years. . . . I am afraid of him. Geri, the deputy city manager is just like him and they hired Sharon as an assistant city manager with no skills. . . . We are lost!"

After three years, twenty-five managers had left the organization for different companies and cities, feeling less competent in their skills, less sure of their ability to manage, and less comfortable with whom they were. Remember, the city council said Leland was doing a great job. Maybe it was the managers. Maybe it was no longer a good fit. Maybe they were out of touch.

Audrey is a human resources director in a Fortune 500 corporation. She has been with the company as director for fifteen years. Recently, executive leadership changed hands, and Audrey was confronted with her political arch rival at the throne of leadership. Audrey was petrified. In meetings with the new chief executive officer, she was told, "You do what I say, or you will be out of here in a heartbeat. I will make you pay for all the things you have done to me over the last ten years!" Audrey was trapped by her desire to maintain her potential retirement income. She determined that she would "suck up her gut" and take whatever he was going to dish out.

One year has past and Audrey can no longer take the stress of the situation. He has shamed her in front of her staff, called her incompetent, reduced her responsibilities, and gotten the board of directors to agree with his changes. Audrey goes into the hospital with a diagnosis of acute depression. The organization continues under the same leadership.

Larry is a former manager of employment with a major utility. When Larry was hired by the utility, he was touted as the most visionary, follow-through manager within the organization. He rose quickly, becoming director of human resources, then executive assistant to the general manager. Over three years, he enjoyed success with employees, who stated that he was a caring and responsive manager.

Larry was demoted one day by the general manager without discussion to his original position of manager of employment. The rumor mill was buzzing with the news, and Larry felt shamed by the actions of the general manager. He needed the job to pay his bills yet, confused by the nondialogue that occurred around the action, resented the embarrassment that had been caused by the demotion. Larry became unresponsive to employees and co-workers. He began to come to work at eight in the morning and leave at five in the afternoon promptly. What the organization used to get in energy was gone. He would stay in his office and talk with no one. He felt shamed by the executive and felt the organization participated in the shame.

Each of these examples are true situations that have occurred within the past eighteen months in organizations. A variety of strategies can be employed to assess the previously described situations. Anne Wilson Schaef, co-author of *The Addictive Organization,* speaks of these actions as components of an addictive personality and addictive organization. She states that "confusion, self centeredness, dishonesty, perfectionism, control, ethical deterioration and crisis orientation are central to addictive behavior." For Schaef, organizations become addictive personalities that have taken a global perspective. She states that

The addictive system fosters dishonesty at every turn. . . . On a national level we can see self centeredness operating in our foreign policy. Everything happening in the world is seen as either for or against the United States. . . . Everything is viewed within our interests. . . . Confusion prevents us from taking responsibility and keeps us ignorant from what's going on. . . . These organizations thrive on crisis and hardly know how to function when things are normal. . . . Perfection means always knowing the answer. The addictive system actually assumes that it is possible to be perfect therefore if you buy into perfection, you establish a pattern of failure. . . . A major preoccupation of the addictive system is control, or the illusion of control. . . . The addictive system harbors a belief that it is possible to control everything. . . . Because of this illusion, addicts have to deal with frozen feelings, being totally out of touch with what is really going on. . . . The inability to feel sets up dysfunctions.

The premise of her approach is that all organizations become addictive when managers are unwilling to embrace the humanity within them. As managers detach from humanity, the organization is unable to recognize the need for the humanness necessary in the decision making. Businesses promise that change will occur, that life will be better, and that the actions are for the good of all, while, ultimately, incremental change leads to no change at all. The dysfunction is perpetuated and the loss of change becomes a bind that blocks the organization and its leaders from being honest. Rationalization becomes the norm.

In *Organizational Violence: Creating a Prescription for Change,* I speak of the creation of superimposed violence paradigms that occur when organizations and their leaders discount the tenets of violence. The tenets of violence are as follows:

1. The inability of people and organizations to effectively create bonds that foster collaboration and inclusiveness

2. The inability of people and organizations to place a high value on inclusiveness in sharing among people the process of growth and understanding regarding the desired outcomes of organizations

3. The inability of people and organizations to balance the need for individuality with the work ethic of team performance

4. The inability to embrace rather than discount the introduction of ideas and ideals

5. The inability to resolve issues of control, power, and authority
6. The inability to assess life's dichotomies where choices are made regarding ends justifying the means versus the means being a critical dynamic towards achieving an appropriate and just end

The premise of the theory is that integrity is fundamental to every business and every business decision—private, public, or nonprofit. Without the ethical perspective, organizational violence can become the norm of business operations.

John H. Jackson and Cyril P. Morgan, authors of *Organization Theory: A Macro Perspective for Management,* state

The study of people in organizations is a proper and vital study for managers and administrators because organizations are more than an aggregation of individuals. These aggregations of people take on their own characteristics, therefore one must study the people and the system. . . . Structure, rules and organizational norms are equally influenced by the people who lead. Because organizations are a unit of analysis separate and apart from the psychology of organization members, the examination of the two is critical to overall organizational success.

Business must take into consideration organizing, the process of organizing, societal conditions, time in history, organizational niche, life cycle crises of people and the systems, and growth stages of the people.

If analysis does not embrace both the systems in operation and the people accountable for the operations, then no analysis will be valuable for the future of organizations.

These two theorists postulate that a balance between the systems and the people is critical. Without that balance, the effective decisions, actions, and choices are not possible.

The issue for business leaders is to focus as equally on the impact of their choices as they have focused on the intent of their choices. In all three situations spoken of in the beginning of this chapter, little thought was given to the impact of the decision on the employee. Self-centeredness and control were the intents of the actions, and shame and discount were the impacts of the choices made. Too often, the business decision is predicated on a personal need that has control and self-centeredness as the real intents. Shame becomes the real legacy for the business.

Consider your decisions as managers and leaders. Assess the ethical choice being made. Determine where perfection, control, self-centeredness, dishonesty, and ethics factor into the decision-making process. If these factors are components of the decision, then recognize that shame is a likely outcome for the recipient of the decision.

Whether the action surrounding a project deals with changes in fiscal reporting, involves development of a marketing strategy, or is another business choice, shame is a realistic outcome.

THE NATURE OF SHAME

Shame is the systematic discounting of a person's value and promise that binds the individual to a belief that existence and personal influence is no longer a viable option for mastering change and altering perspectives that others individually and collectively have of the person. The process of invalidation that accompanies shame makes it difficult, if not impossible, for individuals and systems to make a difference in the participating in or changing the order of the organization. Previously I spoke of closed systems. Invalidation is a critical component of the closed system and shame is the controller of that system.

Consider a new recruit in a police department. The new recruit works from a value system that all citizens of the community should be treated with respect. Upon entry into the system, it becomes apparent to the new recruit that the police system values a hierarchy of citizens that should be followed to ensure that the historical order remains the same. Valued by the police system, in order, are rich persons, white persons, Asian persons, Hispanic persons, African-American persons, and Native or First American persons. In order for the recruit to become a part of the system, he or she is pressured to assimilate the values of that system. Over time, invalidation of the recruit's belief system becomes evident, and the recruit loses a sense of self in order to belong. The same is true within corporations. Corporations, as closed systems, invalidate the beliefs and the ideas that are often brought to the system by new initiates. The process of invalidation, in order to belong to the system, establishes a process of shame. Do as the system believes or get discounted. Move through the system as the system believes or be shamed out, and blamed as an incompetent.

Recently, a human resources department within a major utility exemplified the blame and shame process. The organization was used to dictating human resource changes and codifying the changes, albeit inappropriate, to create structures, avoid personnel-related actions, or violate policies. When the new director of human resources came on board, she tried to craft a system that allowed for equitable treatment of all persons impacted by the system. The system did not like the desired changes, and began to identify and search for incidents of choices that would allow them to discount, invalidate, and oppose any changes made to the history of the organization. They used a process of external referencing by invalidating the value and competence of the internal staff, and hired consultants to validate their historical view. Employees within the human resources department felt shamed, blamed, discounted, frustrated, confused, and disillusioned by the actions of the organization. Oppositional defiant behavior became the outcome, and the organization was able to discount the employees even more, stating their lack of professionalism and dishonest behavior. The addictive process of blame and shame was established. This practice of shaming occurs daily throughout public and private life, and the fragmentation and compartmentalization of decision making and choice continues.

THE CULTURE OF SHAME AND BLAME

Ralph Thomlinson, a professor of sociology at California State University of Los Angeles, stated in his book, *Sociological Concepts and Research: Acquisition, Analysis and Interpretations of Social Information,* that "norms are the rules in the game of life. Techniques, folkways, mores and laws are the governing rules that guide culture and action. Techniques are the manner or strategies that people use to function, folkways are the correct manner of doing things, mores are like folkways with the addition of moral values attached to the correctness of ideas and laws are the formal means of social control made explicit through codification."

People violate these norms daily and pay the price of violation through blame and shame. When you do not meet the norms, then you are restricted in the strategies and in the value that you have for the organization. In experiencing the changes, the culture of the organization is molded and codified for all to see. Consider the care of a lawn in Las Vegas. The technique component of the social norms involves whether you use a power mower or a hand mower to establish your pattern of cutting the lawn. The folkway of the system is that lawns must be cut once a week and that it should be the man of the house who performs the cutting ritual. The mores are violated if the weeds are allowed to go higher than three inches. The laws state that water can never run in the street, and that watering can only occur during the hours of six in the evening and seven in the morning. Everything is fine as long as everyone follows the rules and the rules can be broken as long as everyone else in the community agrees with the breaking of the rules. However, one individual who follows the rules can become upset and report the violations to the police, and the game has changed. This process of following the rules of the organization are evident every day. Employees within organizations are constantly challenged to understand the rules and norms without a clarity regarding the value of the norms in place. Violation of the norms establishes a pattern of shame and blame that devalues the work and the need for the employee within the organization. As you consider your path to success, consider the norms you embraced in order to succeed, and the costs to your personal value system and your personal functioning.

SOCIALIZATION

Socialization of members of an organization is the process through which an individual is molded into a social being through learning to think and behave according to the values and norms prevalent in the organization. Attitudes, habits, and other attributes comprising the personality of an effective member of the organization are based on the extent of the socialization and the ability of new members to comply with the rules of the organization. If one can internalize the norms of the organization, then one is accepted, and moves through the process of inclusion in a rapid fashion. If one is unsuccessful in the internalization process, one finds that isolation and detachment are the results of the cultural process.

THE COURTSHIP OF CORPORATE AND PUBLIC LIFE

I was recently rereading a book entitled *Uncommon Therapy*, by Jay Haley, regarding courtships in personal relationships, and was struck by the similarities to people in corporate life. Haley implies that fear is a critical component of the socialization and courtship process. He believes that individuals in dating recognize the traps that impede the development of relationships, and "put on their best face" to ensure that the relationship continues beyond a first meeting. Although fear is prevalent, the behaviors of the persons in the relationship do not mirror the internal feeling. As I look at the behaviors of employees in the workplace, it is apparent that decisions have been made that allow employees to enter the workplace, with all its fears of socialization, inclusion, rules, and regulations, fearing the consequences of imperfection (an addictive function), yet displaying no fear of the organization. The disconnect between the person and the actions of the person to belong suggest that the person is trapped by a more and folkway of how one is to act versus attachment to the internal fears that might become real information for altering the decisions that perpetuate dysfunctional organizational and personal action.

Organizations want all employees to be effective. Stephen Covey, in his book, *The Seven Habits of Highly Effective People*, says that people must get to the point that they experience the "aha" in order to alter the experiences they find that torment their minds, actions, and souls. The more bound the person is by the ineffective mores, laws, and folkways, the more significant the "aha" when it triggers the need for a paradigm shift. Covey states that effectiveness is based on key principles that guide personal and organizational functioning. Integrity, human dignity, service, quality, potential, growth, patience, nurturance, and encouragement are each critical to effectiveness in the workplace and personally. None of these principles speak to control, groupthink, adherence to rules, historical action, or thought. Each of these principles speaks instead to embodying and empowering activities that allow businesses to function effectively, and to the potential of the organization and the person to bring to the organization their history and their being.

Socialization into the existing organizational culture is altered to consistently and continually create an open, rather than a closed, organizational system. Blame is created when only the history is allowed. Shame is created when only the established practices of the system can be tolerated. Decisions that bind, are fragmented to a given outcome, are compartmentalized (only looking at the historical methods of implementation and codification), that mandate compliance rather than development, or foster and mandate control and obedience are decisions that trap and tear us apart.

THE NATURE OF CHANGE

This chapter focuses on the traps that tear us apart. Throughout the first two parts of this book, I have approached organizational and business functioning from a psychodynamic–deterministic strategy. I sense that business as a living metaphor is bound by the same issues of humanity that attract clinicians to the study of human behavior. As living organisms, businesses are framed by the decision-making theories that often frame human behavior and thought, thus making it critical that business consider realistically the full range of humanity in the success of choices that govern business action.

Psychological development, business development, organizational development, and change are all bound by a need to ensure that all facets of decision making embody and empower persons to bring to the organization excellence, integrity, quality, potential, and wholeness. The business process demands a sense of wholeness and wellness that is predicated on the potential of humans to blend what is equitable and fair with clear competition that often addresses market share, not product quality. Product quality must include the human condition, or product and service will falter.

THE ADJUSTMENTS WE MAKE TO BELONG

John is the general manager of a major utility. He prides himself on being an effective manager of change, yet seems to make all decisions based on the fiscal strength or tight management control effect on the business. He rarely seems to look at the human condition, and in crafting change, often disempowers and instills fear in the managers and employees of his organization.

His process of managing violates every tenet of this author's perspective of organizational violence as described in the book, *Organizational Violence: Creating a Prescription for Change.* In the book, I stated that "in evaluating organizational performance, organizations must realize that success goes beyond the completion of a project. Organizational success must be balanced by assessing the health of the employees and the organizational congruence of policies, procedures and practices along with the outcomes of any projects. Fiscal health and success must be balanced with adherence to organizational ideals. Successful growth and development can only be long term when policies and goals mirror the actions of an organization's officers toward a given end."

As leader of his organization, John was expected to guide organizational behavior and establish a framework for growth and development of the people to the values and principles of the organization and its underlying mission of water and wastewater quality. He focused on water and wastewater, and discounted the real needs of the employees for stability and equity in their treatment. Managers felt continually blamed and shamed by his actions, employees felt invalidated by his decisions, socialization was a process of fear, and external referencing was the only valid determinant for any work performed internally by staff. The continual discount and emotional abuse created psychotic, manic-depressive and conduct disorder actions throughout all the tiers of the organization.

John was terminated as general manager because of his failure to consider the human condition. He was a nice person, and was effective in his business decisions that impacted fiscal and product matters for the business. He just forgot about the people, and the people brought about his professional demise. They believed that people were more important than things, and a price for the invalidation was extracted.

Consider one final thought as we move to what works effectively for organizational development and business decision making. All of business decision making can be considered an adjustment disorder management process. An adjustment disorder is a reaction to an identifiable psychosocial (or multiple stressors) that occurs within three months of the onset of the stressor. Maladaptive reactions are framed by (1) impairment in occupational functioning or social relationships, (2) symptoms that are in excess of a normal and expectable reaction to the stressor, (3) disturbances that are not a one-time pattern of overreaction to the stressor, and (4) the maladaptive reaction lasting longer than six months. The *Diagnostic Statistical Manual IV* describes adjustment disorders in categories of anxious mood, depressed mood, disturbance of conduct, mixed disturbance of emotions and conduct, physical complaints, with-drawal, and work inhibitions. Each of these issues describes situations that have gotten out of hand to the extent that the individual is unable to manage the external influences that arise, causing a disturbance in the normal order of a life's experiences. With this definition, businesses must consistently include the human condition in all decisions if they hope to achieve success with the business goals. Finances, revenue streams, and product success are all external business stressors that of-ten impact the human condition within an organization. Only through a concerted effort to include the human condition will businesses ex-perience their decisions as effective and long lasting.

ORGANIZATIONAL CODEPENDENCE

CHAPTER

6

A Commonplace Activity

Recently, I met with forty of my clients regarding changes and alterations within their corporations and governments. Topics for the time together focused on executive mental health and organizational codependence. The dynamics of the discussion surrounded the potential of organizations and organizational leaders to slip back into modes of behavior and action that limit and inhibit growth that initially began during the times of intervention. A side benefit was the mingling of executives, who were unfamiliar with one another, and their common concerns and views about organizational management and leading a business.

Some of the comments from the conference are summarized for your consideration here. David is the chief executive officer of a small computer firm. He reported, "It's difficult to maintain a momentum toward positive change when you get trapped in fixing all the problems that arise on a day-to-day basis." Mark, the president of a hospital corporation, said, "I understand, whether you are large or small, you find that your survivability is based on reducing the real problems that arise, in spite of all your good intentions." Joyce, the senior executive manager for a major publishing house, said, "It doesn't matter what I want to do, I am controlled often by the situation or by the actions of my competitors. This is such a cut-throat business that you have to mirror what your competitors do and make the people come along." Libby, the director of a health maintenance organization, said, "In reality, We are just as trapped as our people are, and we lose sight of strategies that we plan to respond to the immediate crisis on a daily basis. Sure, we have the strategies out there, but sticking to them doesn't work when you have to respond to the whims of a board of directors!"

The comments from each of these executives indicate the plight and the humanity of the executives who run America's corporations. American business is caught in a codependent cycle. Our business culture mandates that executives and their corporations become living examples of accountability for the actions, thoughts, fears, angers, self-esteem, repressions, obsessions, and blames of our society and the people in it. Taking responsibility, being accountable, and growing and developing on your own are foreign words in this continuing society. Our leaders are expected to be caretakers of the corporations and inevitably become trapped by the behaviors they are expected to assume for the sake of the organization. Consider the following behaviors of caretakers:

1. They think and feel responsible for other people. They are held accountable for other people's feelings, choices, wants, needs, and well-being.
2. They feel they are required to help and solve the issues of others, offering unwanted advice or determining solutions without allowing others to develop needed skills to help themselves.
3. They find themselves saying yes to boards of directors when they want to say no. They find themselves doing things they do not want to do, often doing more than their fair share.
4. They try to please others rather than themselves.
5. They overcommit themselves.
6. They feel stressed and pressured and blame others for the spot they are in.

Executives have become corporate caretakers, unable to maintain healthy behaviors because of the demands established by the organization. As caretakers, they often project an aura of high self-esteem, when in actuality, low self-esteem is the norm. They got to be executives because they could conform to a set of norms established by others that discounts and denies the presence and needs of the executive for the needs of the organization. As persons usually straddled with lower self-esteem, these executives get angry and defensive, and sometimes self-righteous and indignant, when anyone blames them or criticizes them for their actions or decisions. They often become depressed because others do not respect or praise them for their hard work, take things personally, and fear rejection. In their fear of rejection, they often establish patterns of emotional disconnect from the actions around them—perpetuating the situations of rejection. Sometimes they feel like victims and work more diligently to prove themselves to self and others.

Repression and obsession are often outcomes in the codependent state. Pushing thoughts and feelings out of cognitive reality because of fear and guilt is a common action of executives who repress feelings and thoughts. They often never find answers and no problem is ever finished. Revisiting decisions is also a common action. People are not to be trusted by codependents; therefore, codependent executives are always trying to catch the employee in some act of misbehaving and wonder why they have difficulty getting things accomplished. Sometimes, these executives find themselves focusing on controlling others by becoming very control oriented. They become workaholics; and in so doing, their communication skills and patterns become strategies of blame, threatening, coercing, begging, bribing, never saying what they mean, and asking for what they need in indirect patterns. They talk about other people, say nothing is their fault (or everything is their fault), and begin to talk in cynical and hostile ways.

Codependents ultimately do not trust themselves or others. They do not trust their decisions, feelings, or other people and often feel scared, angry, and hurt. Some executives with whom I have worked feel that if they display anger, people will go away. They often punish people for making them angry and usually give employees one chance. If you make a mistake, your professional career within that organization is over because the codependent executive never forgives another for mistakes or actions that might hurt him or threaten his professional existence.

Each of the behaviors previously spoken of in this chapter speak of the extremely negative behaviors resident in the actions of the executive. However, consider these behaviors that executives and boards of directors enjoy, and think of how often these behaviors are projected on to the employees within an organization. Codependent executives and leaders can be extremely responsible, or become martyrs, sacrificing their personal lives and families for the good of the organization. They often vacillate in decisions to ensure that all parties and issues have been considered before they make a decision, and often stay very loyal to their beliefs and actions, repeating them in situations and organizations throughout their life, building a consistent pattern of performance. Sometimes they will lie and cover up the problem for the sake of the organization.

In each of these situations, we have unhealthy leaders who need to embrace the behaviors learned early in life that impact their ability to lead effectively for the present and future. Businesses must focus as much energy on creating health and wellness as they focus on the development of a new product or service for entry into society.

THE CASE OF THE CODEPENDENT EXECUTIVE AND THE CODEPENDENT ORGANIZATION

Robert is the former senior manager of a state mental health system. Robert's first job within the mental health system was that of a management analyst. For three years he watched the actions of the managers around him, and determined that their professional progression was slowed because they were unable to identify the needs of the system and fulfill those needs. Robert worked for two more years developing political connections. He was successful in the connections because he could identify what the politician needed and supply it, regardless of the impact on others around him.

Within one year, Robert was promoted to manager of the grants management division of the state mental health system. He worked diligently to provide for the needs of the organization; in fact, he was perceived as a valued manager because of his tireless dedication to the organization. Robert had total involvement in his work with a limited social life. He neglected his old friends and his former hobbies. He was preoccupied with the behaviors of others and dependent on the political leaders to approve of his behavior and worth to the organization. Robert was protective of his turf and his feelings. It did not matter what he was asked to do—he found a way to accomplish that work, even when performing the task was an anathema to his value system and his belief structure. Whatever the need of the organization, it surpassed his own needs and the needs of his family. As long as he performed in the same ritualistic manner, he would be valued by the organization.

Robert had become addictive and codependent to the organization. He could not see it and the payoffs from the organization were extensive. Within ten years, he had become the assistant director of mental health. Unknowingly, other managers took their cue from Robert's behavior, and the addictive structure that Robert had created was now the norm of the organization, guiding organizational behavior and organizational culture.

Robert survived in the system for a total of fifteen years. Robert died of a stroke and heart attack one afternoon in May three years ago. Everyone at the funeral said, "It's too bad about Robert. He was a good man." He was replaced in seventeen hours by Grant, his protégé. People talked about Robert for two months and then his name was forgotten. No gold watch, no plaque on the wall, no program named for all of his hard work—nothing. Robert was forgotten, and Grant began to create his own stamp on the organization, using the skills and techniques he had learned from Robert.

These actions are replayed every day in corporate America in government, industry, technology firms, sales organizations, consulting firms, and academic institutions. The process of organizational codependence is alive and well throughout our society. You might want to ask yourself the following questions regarding your organization. As you ask the questions, consider whether the actions of your company breathe life into the organization or strip the organization of life. As you ponder the questions, look at your own behavior and determine whether you perpetuate organizational codependence or find yourself on the outskirts of the organization. Consider whether your organization supports independence, or whether codependence is the organizational paradigm.

1. How was I oriented to the company? Were the values and beliefs of the organization and its culture identified? Was I given boundaries that were a blend of my strengths and the organization's need?

2. How did I learn what was acceptable within the organization? Was fear the predominant learning module, or was trust? Did people warn me regarding what was acceptable, and did I find myself becoming skeptical of the platitudes given in the orientation process?

3. Was blame a critical behavior within the organization? Were mistakes allowed, or were people not forgiven? Was a paradigm of violence the norm rather than a paradigm of trust?

4. Have I changed for the better since coming to the company or have I become like everyone else within the firm? Do I do things to get ahead that often hurt others or even one person? Is my personal success a consistent justification for my actions?

5. Has the company changed, or is the company losing critical skilled personnel because of the behaviors within the organization?

6. Is absenteeism up in the organization? Are health care costs rising? Are unions being created where they did not exist before? Are managers complaining more than they used to?

Consider these thoughts as you consider your answers. I am not just talking about the leader or executive. Codependence is a creeping disease, creeping up on us without any clear notification. It begins with poor communication patterns or poor decisions within the organization. It occurs when we walk in the organization and are infected by someone who has ill feelings about how employees are treated. It occurs when people talk about cultural change, yet work hard to maintain the current culture through the incremental process of change. It occurs when we see someone treated poorly and say nothing about it. It occurs when we see relationships changing the equity dynamics of organizational decision making. It creeps into our lives and, over time, we embrace the dysfunction and perpetuate it because of the benefits of compensation, organizational placement and movement, and organizational power received by participating in the addictions.

People and systems are not very different—in fact, people and systems are never separated. One creates the other. Remember in Chapter 1, I talked of the process of choice. The process of choice is a continuum of understanding the path of getting from point A to Z, and dictates whether we move through the organizational life as a healthy contributing member of the organization, or as a codependent, unhealthy perpetuator of organizational dysfunction. The process of choice causes you to limit and narrow options that allow you to move within an organization. If your choices are to maintain personal values, the choice may cause you to go only so far within the organization. If your choice is to integrate the values of the organization, you may find that you move through the organization, but your discounting and selective adoption process impacts your decision making. One strategy supports inclusion and holism; the other compartmentalization, fragmentation, and detachment. Remember the dynamics of choice, focusing on emotions, feelings, beliefs, history, culture, gender, and development. Dynamics of choice will cause you to select roles and options that lead to a specific end. We play out that end and we protect that role.

Remember Robert, the mental health director. He played out a role within the organization as the consummate "yes" man in spite of who it hurt, and the organization used him to the end. His approach was antagonistic to people but supportive of the organization. Remember, antagonism breeds blaming strategies and defeats inclusiveness. Robert didn't want inclusion. Robert wanted total organizational power.

Remember dissonance of choice as you consider your behaviors within organizations. Has there been a level of congruence within the organization based on the decisions made? Has there been personal congruence, or have you bought into actions in order to survive within the organization? Remember that dissonance fragments and tangents compartmentalize development and organizational action. Which have you experienced?

Robert is not an abstract example of leaders—he is more the norm than the exception. I remember my own actions as a human resources executive. I diligently worked to achieve the organization's missions and dreams. I focused on the problems and worked seventy hours a week to achieve the outcomes of the organization. I believed that if I worked diligently, a let-up would occur somewhere down the line and planned action would take over. How wrong I was. The more I did, the more the organization found to resolve, and the more codependent I became to the organization's process of control and dysfunction. The creeping disease was upon me. The patterns of choice were evident through a consistent internal pattern of "burn one up and throw them away."

THE IMPACTS OF THE ORGANIZATION PROCESS

Throughout this process of exploration and discovery, people make choices. The choices are made based on the emotional makeup and beliefs of the person and their willingness to risk within the organizational environment. Rarely can one say, "I didn't have a choice!" We all have choices, and we often avoid looking at the impact of the choice on us—just as organizations rarely look at the total picture in the choices they make. People and systems have become compartmentalized, fragmented, detached, and discounted entities, struggling to survive in a societal system that focuses on fiscal outcomes more than outcomes that responsibly consider the participants and recipients. Certainly, there is due care for the accuracy of the product, the quality of the service, the cost of the development, and the profits achieved; however, rarely is the concern and care extended to the process utilized to get to the end.

The impact of the organizational process is equally, if not more, important as the product or service provided. The people who performed in the first process are always needed for the second. If they have been damaged in the first process, then getting the best from them in the second go-around is less likely.

Looking to the end often causes organizations and organizational leaders to reflect realistically only on the history that has been successful within the organization and has gotten the leader to the top of the organization. Process is culture, and any change, new development, or new thought cannot be accomplished using the old rules of the organization or the old strategies for development and implementation. Culture must continually change and the processes must change. Therefore, the strengths and skills that each person brings to the process can significantly enrich it for the organization and its members.

Price Pritchett and Ron Pound wrote in *High Velocity Culture Change*, "Instead of wasting precious time contemplating the organization's navel, trying to sort out precisely what the existing culture is, simply get clear on what it needs to be. . . . Do things that help the culture change. Attempts at incremental change—'tweaking' the culture—ordinarily die for lack of energy. If you try to go slow, bureaucracy and resistance to change will cancel out your efforts."

CONTROL AS THE UNFORTUNATE OUTCOME

Both Parts One and Two of this book have been about choices that control. The task for the future of living businesses is freeing the people and opening the systems to embrace real change and growth. Real impact is based on our ability to embrace freedom. Introspection therefore becomes a critical need without it becoming a navel exercise.

We are at the nexus of transforming who we are and what we can become. Certainly, remaining in the past discussed here is not a healthy strategy, so going forward must be the only real course. Control perpetuates a closed organizational system that binds development and examination. Each time you perpetuate a closed system, you limit the potential for change and development. Each time the closed system gets hold of the organization, dysfunctions of manic depression and personality dysfunction become more pronounced within the organization. Each time control dictates action and thought, conduct disorders and oppositional defiant disorders become the new strategies within the organization, building a norm of codependence.

MINI-EPILOGUE

Looking at the Traps of Life That Impact Business Decision Making and Corporate Being

"If true commitment to the people and the society is to occur, then at some point a theory of transforming action must be crafted to ensure that the illusions of power and control are not perpetuated. Without a transforming strategy, dysfunctions run rampant and all of society loses!"
—*Dr. Lloyd C. Williams, Consultant and Author,*
given at the Convocation on Organizational Violence,
San Francisco City College, 1995

There is an inherent issue within business encompassing the ability of business to transform itself to the everchanging climate of open versus closed business. The closed business system is the traditionally framed approach to an industrialized society that tightly structures work, product development, marketing, sales, human resource management, and fiscal responsibility. This closed system defines tightly all the parameters of how business is accomplished and how decision making is framed. The structure is a tiered process that requires leaders and employees to embrace a "parental" model of organizational management. This model is punitive in structure and says that humans are to be told what is allowable in the structured organizational society. From this framework comes the current societal imperatives driving business decision making. Where as a holistic approach requires trust as an underlying paradigm, current organizational wisdom modifies and says, "I trust you as long as you do it my way." That framework is a paradoxical system that breeds confusion and frustration, demanding of people that they compartmentalize and fragment their thinking and action modalities in order to survive through the maze of dysfunctional communications so prevalent in our business environments.

Recently, I was talking with a young certified public accountant (CPA) regarding his long-range career plans and options. He stated that participation in a public accounting firm was not a viable option because the "barracuda" nature of the CPA business was an anathema to how he saw himself and how he wanted to work in the future. This young CPA had determined that the paradigm in which CPA firms operated was not the paradigm in which he could live and thrive. Thoughts similar to his are held by people throughout the country in their perspectives of government, private industry, nonprofit corporations, and to some extent, academia. No existing system is perfect, and no existing system is truly open in its ongoing approach to business.

Business is choking on its own umbilical cord in the strategies it employs to accomplish short- and long-term business outcomes. It is framing its future based on the strategies of its past, and effectually halves the potential embodied in business to redesign and reframe itself. Business is quick to decide what not to do, and slow to decide what will guide its future.

We are challenged to find a different path. Theorists such as Jack Gibb, Peter Senge, Stephen Covey, Ann Wilson Schaef, Frank Friedlander, Will McWhinney, and countless others have developed varying approaches to the changing business and the changing person. Gibb and Schaef are the two closest to describing the humanity of business and its need to learn from personal development as a strategy for organizational development and change in business. No one has framed the development of business and people as parallel systems of change that balance each other for the present and future. This is the emerging challenge of this book: building parallel paradigms that consider the human condition and the concept of living business. Without that structure, clinical dysfunction is the outcome.

PART III

CREATING THE PARTNERSHIP

TRANSFORMING BUSINESS

7

The Building of Parallel Paradigms That Impact the Business System and the Business Employee

Transforming business can be a monumental, frightening, and rewarding assignment. The assignment is driven by a need to do away with the paradigms of old—crafting paradigms for the present and future that are forever emerging, changing, and challenging the existing data, guiding effective decisions that influence and enrich corporate profits and systems. Transforming decisions require a transformed framework for analyzing and creating decisions. Transforming employees and leaders require transformed values and outcomes for measuring performance that are significantly different from the existing frameworks. Business must change its window of vision if it is to move beyond a closed system to one that is open and fluid.

This is the heart of the transformation theory that frames the thoughts and actions that follow. All of the past must be frozen for us to address what can and must be. Transforming decisions and actions are based on the ability of people and business to recognize the limits of a closed organizational process that tightly frames rules, regulations, norms, and behavior to achieve an outcome. In a tight and closed system, the ability to reflect and respond to changing issues and dynamics becomes a difficult and arduous process. Fluid and open systems are poised to alter components of the system to embrace and include change, rather than fight, resist, and confront it.

Issues of emergence, acknowledgment, disclosure, re-emergence, and self-indulgence become important in the transformational process for people. Issues of equality, interpretation, empowerment, reciprocity, commitment, and representation become important for systems and businesses. Congruence and wholeness become mirror images for the person and business, and set the stage for framing long-term development. In this process, I have created a business paradigm that opens the organization to a new way of thinking about systems.

THE CHANGING BUSINESS PARADIGM

Business development for the present and future can become more effective through altering existing business strategies from a closed systems process to a more open and fluid one. This process requires that business rethink the approach currently used to understand and analyze the decisions that guide the business. If you will remember, in Chapter 1, discussion of the choices that people made was essential to the elements of dysfunction that usually occur in the business process. Table 7.1 focuses on the components of a changed paradigm for thinking and acting in business.

In this paradigm, business focuses on seven critical developmental processes as essential ingredients in effective business planning and implementation of products, services, management of resources, competition, and expansion. Rather than looking at fragmented or compartmentalized

Table 7.1
Paradigm for Business and People Development

People Development	Business Development
Discord	Equality
Emergence	Interpretation
Acknowledgment	Reciprocity
Disclosure	Empowerment
Self-Indulgence	Representation
Re-Emergence	Commitment
Congruence	Wholeness

Note: The process of changing, thinking, and action to process development and integration. The process of development is a dual system of personal and organizational change. Being congruent and whole requires an integration of people and system development.

elements, each element of the paradigm allows the business to frame decisions based on the potential of the decision to impact one of the seven underlying areas of development. Without the decision impacting an element, business must rethink the decision to ensure a level of wholeness with the decision in progress. The paradigm focuses on processes that are integrative and expansive, as well as changing and continuous, rather than any set or static process. The paradigm has no beginning or end, just levels that must be adhered to in order to provide a level of understanding around the choices that we make in the business environment. Dissonances of choice, incidents of choice, and tangents of choice, as described in Chapter 1, are not possible if you ensure that the levels of the business paradigm are understood, followed, and implemented.

This is a total process business system paradigm, with membranes that expand ad infinitum. Closed systems restrict, open systems allow ad infinitum experiences, and fluid systems allow for levels of integrations that cross the boundaries of all systems, and ultimately, all paradigms. That becomes the purpose and thrust of the new paradigm.

BUSINESS SYSTEM OVERVIEW

The business system paradigm comprises seven levels: equality, interpretation, reciprocity, empowerment, representation, commitment, and wholeness. Each is a separate entity framing business, and each is a part of the whole. When businesses make a choice regarding employees, products, services, strategies, competition, marketing, or any other decision, the decision should impact, or be framed by, one of these levels. Businesses never complete a level; rather, the levels are in tandem with one another in a nonstatic and continuous motion. Because there is no beginning or end to a level, there is no possibility for closure of any of the levels, thus creating a continual evaluation and reliability point in the developmental system.

EQUALITY

Equality is the integrous level of the system. It is the constant check and balance point of reviewing the congruity between what a business determines is valuable and the actions of the business to that existing value. If a business states that it values equity between genders, yet compensates one gender more than the other in the same classifications, then there is an inequity in the actions of the business and discontinuity in the values of the system. Equality is out of sync with the behaviors of the business system.

Equality becomes the "little voice in the background" for all decisions. Business leaders and employees are continually challenged to listen to this voice and determine the integrity of the decision. An example can be consultants who espouse a belief in the integrity of all business decisions, yet share with union leaders, "We can get rid of this general manager," on the one hand, and state to the general manager, "If you just play along, we can get the unions to argue with each other enough about your demise and get them to lose their political influence within the organization." There is no equality in the statements by the consultant; rather, there is the antithesis of equality, which is manipulation.

INTERPRETATION

Interpretation is the ongoing recognition that change is occurring. Environmental scans, visioning processes, strategic business modeling, functional outcome assessment, re-engineering designs, strategic planning efforts, downsizing of staffing, eliminations of layers of an organization, and forecasting of future trends are all data sets that must receive interpretations in light of the nature of the business and the existing values of the business.

Interpretations are the moving frameworks of business choice. Every action, planned or unplanned, can be evaluated through the interpretation level with a constant check through the equality level of the system. As long as recognition of the integrity embodied in the choice is mirrored to the changing environment, then businesses maintain a pulse on the emerging dynamics of the choices that are made for the business.

Interpretations are critical and essential to business choice because they represent an acknowledgment of the fluid nature of business remaining competitive in the work world. Who we are as a business is often framed by the changing and emerging world.

Interpretations are also critical because they allow business to remain inclusive in their strategies. Twenty years ago, the inclusiveness of domestic partner benefits would have been inconceivable in business. Today, 447 corporations around the country are inclusive of domestic partners as a lifelong societal action that impacts their business decision making. Thirty years ago, gender-based issues were not as prevalent as today, and interpretations allow business to reframe and rethink old analyses to replace their former decisions with a newer perspective for being and equity.

RECIPROCITY

Reciprocity is the mutual exchange of business action that moves forward and backward in time and action to ensure the ability of the organization to respond to and frame effective business decisions. Reciprocity is the inclusion component of the business system, ensuring that all parties impacted by a given decision are included in the development of the strategies surrounding the decision. It would be easy for people to suggest that reciprocity involves and requires consensus; instead, reciprocity involves exchanges of privileges to achieve equivalency and inclusion.

Businesses must begin to assess the impacts of their decisions rather than just the intents of their decisions. The reciprocity level of the business paradigm is a check and balance to the impact of the decision choice before the decision is finalized. An example could be the implementation of the Omnibus Transportation Employee Testing Act of 1991 for the 7.5 million commercial driver's license holders throughout the United States. The implementation of the act requires that employees in classifications within organizations requiring the commercial driver's licenses for safety-sensitive positions must participate in six drug and alcohol testing programs in order to maintain their positions within the organizations. Employers have good intentions in the development of programs in compliance with the act, but must, however, assess the impact of the programs developed on the employees impacted by the program. Mutual exchange of information, values, beliefs, and strategies for implementation are essential to the reciprocity level of development. With the reciprocity process, underlying paradigms of violence get superimposed on the organizational structure for the future, thereby avoiding impacting other aspects of business and business decision making. Therefore, reciprocity is the emotional balancer of the organization because it requires inclusion to ensure sanity within the organization.

EMPOWERMENT

Empowerment is the training and development component of any business decision. Businesses must ensure that decisions crafted include an assessment of the potential of the decision to increase the skill and influence parameters for employees accountable for development and implementation of the decision. Webster defines *empower* as the giving of official and legal power to others. For every executive, board member, stockholder, employee, or consultant impacted by any business decision, characteristics of systems become a critical and necessary dynamic. Every system involves *elements* (any object, boundary or relation that can be articulated), *boundaries* (any idea that separates the elements), *relations* (any idea that associates the elements of the system—same thought, same shape, same boundary), *cause* (whatever brings the system into focus such as a condition, presence, absence, or issue), and *qualities* (characteristics of the whole that are evident only at the level of the whole). The process of empowering others becomes the nexus point in the process that activates an assessment of the entire system. When businesses empower, they share power and authority. This calls into question the elements, boundaries, relations, and qualities of the system. The constant revision of the system keeps the system open and reduces the overall fear factors that creep into systems development. If you remember from Chapter 6, codependence is the creeping disorder for business, because it restricts and compartmentalizes effective business decision making. Therefore, empowering others reduces the overall potential for codependent action and thought.

Most organizations in business operate from a classic–idealist paradigm. The systems thinking in this paradigm focuses on labeling, describing, and classifying things. Discovery of essential and true form was critical in this paradigm because clarity had to be established and framed—closed, if you will. This model of systems thinking was devoid of a model for understanding and embracing change; therefore, empowerment of others in any organization would go against the grain of the classical systems thinking.

As businesses continued to develop over time, they embraced the dynamic paradigm, or scientific paradigm of system thinking. This is the conventional wisdom paradigm for current business decision making and decision action. In current business, there must be a cause and effect. Without cause and effect, there is no decision to be made. "Why" is no longer an issue of form in business, it has become the antecedent condition for analysis and decision making. This paradigm thinking perpetuates the compartmentalization and fragmentation of current business. In the dynamic paradigm, thoughts, perspectives, and assumptions about the structure of systems rested on the view, and sometimes belief, that the elements of the system were clear and distinct. Fragmenting the process, and only thinking of products, finance, marketing, human resources, cost assessments, and other issues, were viewed from a singular system perspective. Only one aspect of business needed to be addressed. Change, therefore, would occur within the minuscule system rather than any assessment of the whole. Empowerment frustrated the classic and dynamic systems thinking model because it demands a review of the total system.

REPRESENTATION

Representation is the process of ensuring that separate components of the business decision are connected to ensure a purpose. When the system operates, feedback adjusts and controls the performance of the system to be inclusive and comprehensive in the communication of thoughts, ideas, and future practices.

The communication paradigm of the 1930s focused on the concept of efficiency embodied through the purpose of organizations and the intent of organizations. As long as purpose and feedback were possible, organizations and employees would understand the directions and nexus of all actions.

For me, the concept of representation goes beyond the traditional perspective, and focuses on the expansion of boundaries of a system of decision making. Efficiency, formal, and expansion processes are the strategies for linking one part of a system to the other. Representation embodies the traditional communication—field and evolutionary models of systems thinking—and goes beyond. The field model suggests that boundaries of a system are not real, yet it avoids or discounts the values of the individual. The evolutionary model suggests that elements of a system are clearly defined; however, they may change or transform over time. What remains is a clear hierarchy of authority and control in order to reduce the concept of chaos. In effect, the history of systems thinking never changed.

This system of thinking in the new business paradigm suggests that the outcomes identified in all other theories automatically limited and trapped the thinkers and the implementers of the system in actions and thoughts, because it had an end. True systems work more effectively because the process of the system, not the end of the system, is what becomes important. Therefore, the representation level of the business paradigm focuses on ensuring the purpose, as well as the communication of the purpose of the system, and not the end of the system. The end never occurs, only more intriguing and successful strategies for analyzing the issues to effectively develop a decision that is consistent with the system in light of the overall business direction.

COMMITMENT

Commitment is the ongoing agreement to resolve issues and work toward completion of any given business and personal requirement that impacts the overall business decision or outcome. Most systems thinking models discount or avoid the importance of the human dynamic in the business decision process. This new system mandates commitment that focuses on the blending of system and human inclusiveness to achieve any overall organizational outcome.

Commitment is the embodiment of the entrepreneurial spirit and the embodiment of the spiritual or living being within business. Business is a living process when seen in the context of an open system. As business is not static, the potential to "give up" is larger, because no labels or ultimate descriptions exist to frame and define the business. Therefore, the processes of committing to follow through, be involved, give one's all, and "be present, in the clinical sense" are essential to the overall success of business decision making.

The development of a new product, the analysis of a problem, the working to remain inclusive, and the need to integrate and acculturate the varying diversities of people and ideas, all require the process of commitment. The commitment additionally focuses energies toward ensuring the equality, reciprocity, empowerment, representation, and interpretation of the business process and the business decision.

The civil rights movement, the women's movement, the gay/lesbian movement, the international human rights movement, and the environmental movement are all examples of commitment. What is essential about each movement is the awareness that it is an ongoing commitment. Governor Pete Wilson's response societally to eliminate academic and state utilization of the affirmative action policies and practices of organizations is an example of the classic and dynamic systems thinking that is devoid of fluidness and human recognition. Wilson perpetuates the old thinking strategies that continue to fragment and compartmentalize society and thwart the inclusiveness of people and systems. Every time any politician, activist, or social scientist states that a system is complete or that an end has been achieved, there is an adherence to an old model of thinking that discounts the need for unity between people and systems.

Fear tactics continue to divide a nation around issues of race or economics, strive for reorganization or re-engineering of a corporation, press for competition as the end all of business action, disempower, restrict interpretation, and avoid reciprocity, and each is an example of noncommitment to a living model with the expressed desire of closing the systems in operation.

WHOLENESS

We reach the last cyclical level of the new business paradigm. Wholeness is a concerted and dedicated effort to package and review the actions and thoughts of business through a system of regurgitation. To be effective in the systems thinking paradigm of process business thinking, a cyclical approach that is nonstatic is the ultimate level with no end.

Figure 7.1 depicts the total business paradigm where all components are equal and all components are necessary for a "whole" process of thinking and being. The issue in this system is that business must begin to assess the value of humanity as a critical component of the decision-making process. Focusing on properties or qualities of business, or avoiding seeing people as different from the organization, is a critical change from the traditional field theories that have governed the twentieth-century thinking models. Cause and effect are both important, but not primary, in the process of thinking. Again, Governor Wilson, believed

Figure 7.1
The Business Process Paradigm in Motion

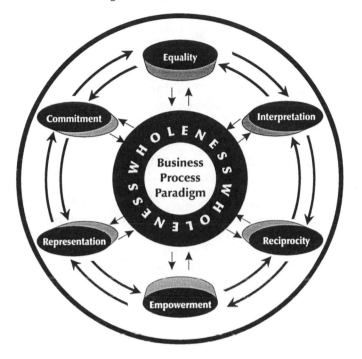

that affirmative action was the cause of the "angry white backlash." He did not look at the process of change and development to see that there was no beginning or end to the sense of equality, reciprocity, or interpretation; rather, there had only been a shift in the thinking parameters that suggested that the old paradigm of cause and effect was no longer working.

The evolutionary paradigm has been the closest to a true transformational paradigm. Will McWhinney is the foremost theorist in this process. He describes systems change as movement to a higher plane of complexity. The belief of McWhinney, in *Paradigms and Systems Theories*, and others is that transformation is based on the ability of the system to respond to more and more complex ideas and issues that confront the system. The second idea of evolutionary thinkers is that change is irreversible. I agree with those premises. However, I find that in the development of this paradigm for business, the decision-making process became more important than the process of reaching a conclusion in the systems process. The process business paradigm's strength is in its continual circle, not the results of any one component of the system.

INTEGRATION OF THE BUSINESS PROCESS
PARADIGM WITH HUMANITY

The second critical strength of the business process paradigm is that it must work in tandem with the human process paradigm displayed in Table 7.1. The process of development is parallel between people and business systems. You will note that people development and business development have similar issues from the titles of the levels of development. Suffice it to say for now, each needs the other, as will be shown later, and each requires similar levels of holism to achieve parity.

THE PEOPLE DEVELOPMENT–HUMAN
PROCESS PARADIGM

Figures 7.2 and 7.3 depict the human process paradigm that exists in the same time and space with the business process paradigm. This system is operational for the entire life span of a human's existence, and provides the framework for human development that is equally nonstatic as the business paradigm is nonstatic.

Figure 7.2
The Human Process Paradigm in Motion

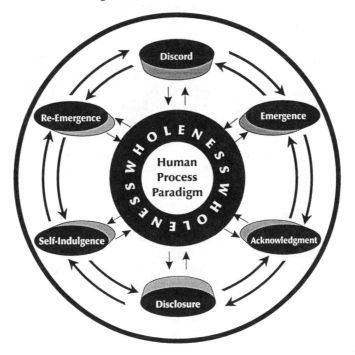

Figure 7.3
The Parallel Paradigms

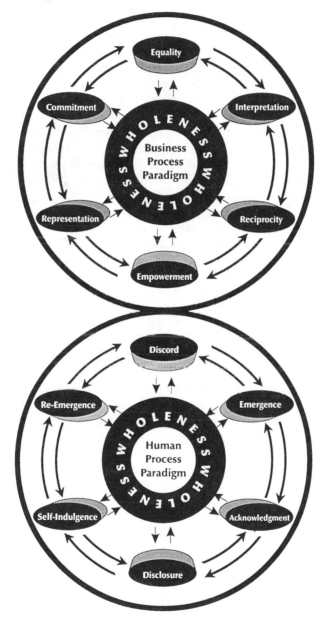

Historically, before psychology and theories of business, there were concepts of purism, nomotheticism, naturalism, and qualitativism. These theories were postulated by Thales, Democritus, and Hippocrates. Over time, theorists such as Plato and Socrates crafted philosophical strategies for the development of a psychology of humanism. Aristotle was the first theorist, however, to postulate a strain of development that focused on early life, middle life, and the need for knowledge from a scientific perspective. Descartes began the process of assessing psychology from a Cartesian perspective, depicted in Table 7.2. As can be seen from the table, theorists throughout time have maintained a linear dualism in assessing the development of people within a cultural context. Over the life of a Cartesian approach to understanding human performance and development, humanity embraces a cultural intent around natural law—a worldview that perpetuates and embodies compartmentalized development as pieces of the whole in the material world, an either–or perspective in the self and other dualism domain, a spatial dimension in the transformation domain, and a cause-and-effect process in the organizing ethos domain. What is unique about the model is the integration of a global linear process that binds and blocks the fluid development of man. Dr. Grant Venerable, a professor of chemistry and African-American studies at San Francisco State University, developed a matrix model of humanity (the Ven Matrix, 1995) that "lays over" parallel systems of development for people, systems, and chemical organizing principles. Dr. Venerable calls this process the "Tripartate Dualism." The focus of the system created is the nonexistence of a beginning or end to the development of humanity. His terminology is rich and expressive when he speaks of "living in harmony with nature, universe as a unified structure of the whole that is greater than the sum of the parts, matter as spirit, people and systems as complementary, holistic, metaphoric, relativistic, universe as God centered." Dr. Venerable has taken the Cartesian approach to psychological and biological development and given it a soul or spirit that has been missing from the developmental theories of human development. It is from that theory that my parallel paradigm of human development grows and expands into a process developmental model that is parallel to the business process paradigm.

THE GIBB MODEL OF PERSONAL AND ORGANIZATIONAL CHANGE

Dr. Jack Gibb, an internationally known clinical and organizational psychologist, looked at the same issues of development in his book, *Trust: A New View of Personal and Organizational Development*, and postulated a congruence model that blended the issues for people and systems.

Table 7.3 depicts the ten-part model in which Dr. Gibb speaks of critical incidents of change for people and systems. The first stage is freedom of flow. In that stage, the healthy organization moves into its own flow with an inner harmony. The second stage is process trusting, where organizations allow the internal processes to operate without over-management or over-control. In the third stage, cognitive–perceptual clarity is critical. The effective system has some shared vision that the members of the system understand. The fourth stage is a humanistic stage, where self-caring is critical. The organization looks at strategies for nurturing itself to maintain its existence. The fifth stage fosters the concept of open systems. Feelings and perceptions are critical in this stage. The sixth stage is one of focused energy. What matters here is the driving force of the organization. In the seventh stage, constraint reduction is important in the organization not being immobilized by its fear. The eighth stage is nurturing environment. In this stage, the internal and external environment of the system lives by the principles of mutuality and cooperation. The ninth stage is in-depth community. The thrust of this phase is the sense or belief of community within the organization. The last phase is the cosmic "allness." This phase is equivalent to Venerable's universe, and my concepts of congruence and wholeness.

The thrust of Gibb's system is that the more an organization emulates trust options, the more the organization mirrors humanity, and in so doing, the healthier the organization becomes. Although I agree in principle with the premise, I find that the concept of "living spirit" is different for people and systems, though they are parallel and work in concert to achieve equivalent outcomes that are ever changing and continually ongoing.

The issue that does exist with Gibb's model is the emphasis given to the organization and the underlying premise that as the organization becomes healthier, so does the person. For years I operated from the premise that if I could help organizations become healthier, then the person would be healthier. I then reversed the premise and worked toward the belief that if I helped individuals become emotionally and clinically healthy, then the organization would in turn become healthier. I eventually realized that both premises were true when used together, but not when used separately.

The clinical perspective is that treating the sick child and sending him back into a sick family system is an anathema to the treatment of the child. The same is true of the organization and the employee. Both must be allowed to heal and become healthy if either is to be healthy. Becoming whole is a process, not an ending system. There is always a growing process that occurs for the person and the system. What is uniquely different is marrying the concept of open systems with healing persons and in so doing, healing and growing personally and organizationally.

Table 7.2
Chemistry and the Optimum System

Comparative Cosmologies (as Idealized Cultural Values)*
LINEAR DUAL vs TRIPARTITE DUAL REALITIES
Socio-Logic Tendencies in Systems Design Ordered by Ven Matrix Domain

---

CARTESIAN - Linear Dualism

Domain "A" - Nature / Natural Law

CULTURAL INTENT
- Dominate / Control nature
- Tendency toward accumulation and exploitation of material and human resources consistent with domination and control

Domain "B" - Material World

WORLD VIEW
- Universe is a vast mechanistic device composed of fixed operating parts, a whole equal to the sum of its parts

ONTOLOGY
- Matter is "real" stuff knowable only through the physical senses. Material constants (image) valued over logical necessity

EXPERIMENTAL METHOD
- "Objectivity" - observing subject split from observed object - no relationship between
- "Technique" - Speed valued often at expense of accuracy (time spent equated with lost money and efficiency)

KEMETIC - Tripartite Dualism

- Live in harmony with nature (Ma'at)
- Tendency toward accumulation and exploitation of material and human resources consistent with Ma'at.

- Universe is a unified, *tripartite* structure of the whole greater than the sum of its parts

- Matter is "spirit," purely an activity, a cosmic illusion -Logical necessity valued over material constants

- "Relative Objectivity" - subject forms relationship with object's reference frame to obtain object's viewpoint
- "Technique" - Slow, deliberate pace valued to not miss small, but possibly crucial details

82

Domain "C" - Self/Other Dualism

SOCIO-CULTURAL ORIENTATION

- Linear (either/or), Male vs female, egoic individuality, competitive, xenophobic, didactic
- Zero-Sum consciousness - Life is win-lose.

EPISTEMOLOGY (framework of knowing)

- Logical-empirical, If A then B causality, fragmentive analysis and resynthesis of the whole

- Specialization, parsimonious deduction of data from general principle; limited induction of the general from specific data.

Domain "D" - Transformation

SYMBOLIC ORIENTATION

- Logical-Digital/Literal-Realism

SPACIO-TEMPORAL CONCEPT

- Newtonian; time is limited, linear in flow, separate from space. Form of change varies with circumstances.

Domain "E" - Organizing Ethos

- Universe is an efficient, utilitarian idea existing to serve the needs of (Judaeo-Christian) man.
- God is a fixed, absolute "first cause" - The CEO of a male hierarchy of middle managers.
- Salvation more dependent upon religious belief than personal conduct.

- Complementary (both/and), male/female harmony, creative individuality, co-operative/group- oriented, xenophilic, dialectic
- (+) Sum consciousness - Life is win-win

- Holistic, Metaphoric, Relativistic - Complementary rationality - Field Causality of sufficient reason - Systemic synthesis; begin with universal and then assign component elements
- Generalization, abstractive induction of universal principles from specific data.

- Analogic-Representational/Relative

- Einsteinian: time is relative and the complement of space; moment is infinite and cyclic. Change seen as cyclic, evolutionary, or instant.

- Universe is a God-centered, transcendent idea.
- God is a universal vibrating energy represented as different facets of nature.
- Salvation more dependent upon personal conduct than religious belief.

Source: Grant D. Venerable, "Chemistry and the Optimum System: On the Tripartate Reality of Afrocentric Science." Proceedings of the Conference of the National Organization for the Professional Advancement of Black Chemists and Chemical Engineers, Los Angeles, 1995.

  * Copyright © 1991–1995, G.D. Venerable

Table 7.3
TORI Trust Model

The theory of model	Statement of the mini-theory
Freedom of flow	The healthy organism moves into its own flow, in tune with its rhythms, with an inner harmony.
Process trusting	The effective organism is one that allows its processes to happen, without over-management, extrinsic motivation, or over-control.
Cognitive-perceptual clarity	The effective system is one in which there is a shared clarity, vision, and mission, viewed and conceived clearly by members who feel the importance of the vision.
Self-caring	The healthy system cares for itself, nurtures its central being, feels its importance, and has a strong sense of identity.
Open system	The effective organism is an open system, with big transparent see-throughable boundaries, and sharing of perceptions and feelings.
Focused energy	The healthy system focuses its energy on what matters. What is central to the flow?
Constraint reduction	The effective organism is free from undue constraint and congesting fears; has a feeling of freedom.
Nurturing environment	The internal and external environment of the effective system is nurturing and fostering of mutuality and cooperation.
In-depth community	The healthy system "feels like" a community, whose members care about the community and each other.
Cosmic allness	The high-trust system senses its allness, its mystical core, and its eternity in the moment.

Source: Jack Gibb, Trust: A New View of Personal and Organizational Development (Los Angeles: Guild of Tutors Press, 1978).

THE HUMAN PROCESS PARADIGM IN MOTION

The human process paradigm shown in Figure 7.2 depicts a fluid system that has no beginning or end. The focus of the system is that people are thrust into a developmental process that demands that issues of discord, emergence, acknowledgment, disclosure, self-indulgence, re-emergence, and congruence are fluid processes that guide the development of people. Early life, middle life, and old age are not the foci of the development process; rather, it is what one understands or does during their development that matters in the creation of a whole or congruent person. Married to the business paradigm, the congruence of the person is equal to the wholeness of the business system.

DISCORD

Discord is the internal development of persons from birth through adolescence. In this time frame of spatial development, lack of clarity surrounding role identity, gender understanding, sexual identity, career identity, relationship development, and other traditional developmental models are the predominant structures. People go through life without clarity in form or structure. Who we are, how we behave, what we understand as morality, what we understand as law, and how we frame that understanding in crafting internal rules are the focuses of this process.

Discord represents the continual internal struggle and challenge to understand one's place in society, personally and professionally. The struggle to recognize one's niche drives the continual discord within the person to put limits and structures on one's self, to reduce the internal chaos that everyone experiences developing. Discord is neither positive or negative; rather, it just exists as the framework of the development of people. Development of strength, internal focus, and coping strategies are all components of the process paradigm in the cycle of living.

What is wonderful about this paradigm process is the realization that businesses and people are always changing and the challenge is developing blend processes for people to focus on their living as businesses must begin to focus on their living. No set pattern is right or wrong; rather, they all exist to mutate or continually change as tantamount to having purpose societally and personally.

Look at the changes crafted by the United Way in the aftermath of the debacle around the use of fiscal resources by the former chief executive officer. The United Way reaffirmed both its commitment to the development of people and its commitment to be clearer in its approach to business. Discord existed within the ranks of the employees because they recognized the taking for granted of givers to the institution and their responsibility to "right livelihood" in order to empower and impact society. The business recognized its role toward wholeness, and significantly altered its business practice to consider issues of equality, reciprocity, interpretation, and commitment. The processes experienced by the United Way were creations of a living spirit within the corporation for the business and the employees. The process of living and developing as parallel concerns became the synergies for continual living for both the corporation and the employees. Keith Green, an employee of the United Way at the Long Beach, California, branch said, "You know, I wasn't really afraid after the fall of the United Way. I actually felt that it gave us a chance to achieve our mission, and it gave me a personal challenge to balance who I am with what I do. I was actually excited." Process paradigms in motion allowed the employee and the system to build respectfully upon one another. Process paradigms in motion moved the discord to the emerging process.

EMERGENCE

Emergence is the flooding of the mind and body with new images, thoughts, and feelings that suggest that change is imminent within the human being. As an adolescent, the emergence stage begins for girls as they experience their first period, and for boys as they enter puberty. For adolescents in college, it could be emerging realization of a passionate field, or the first sexual experience that empowers and connects a boy or girl to one another. For gays and lesbians, it becomes the emerging feelings of communion with another of the same sex. It could be the birth of a child with couples, or the changing in the body from a virile strong person to someone less strong and self-assured. Throughout life, emergence is a critical and constant process.

Emergence is the beginning of comfort with discord because it creates clarity regarding the issues and perspectives that influenced and controlled the discord phase of development. In the emergence cycle, light bulbs go off in the mind regarding issues that created depression and frustration in the discord phase of development. Feelings of connection, joining, comfort, awareness, and self-assuredness because of clarity are the essential dynamics of the emergence phase.

Employees sense the emergence when they give up fear in the organization, or when they recognize that they can exclaim personal power over their own lives and careers. Employees sense the emergence when they stop blaming themselves for the actions of the organization or when they realize that doing their best does not involve castigation of the self. Whenever one recognizes that continuation of the discord phase is not essential to growth and development, then emergence is free to nurture and enhance the development of the person.

Emergence also frees and empowers the person to search for others with similar experiences and views, creating the joining and group process of development. Communication—listening, sharing, participating, and framing perspectives—occurs during the emergence stage. An excellent example is the emerging development of gay and lesbian persons in their "coming out" stage of development. For the gay or lesbian, emergence is a process of acceptance of one who is without criticism or guilt. Being whole is a recognition of the existence of feelings and differences without fear of reprisal. For African-Americans and Hispanics, the same dynamics are evident, as they exclaim who they are with a history of thought that does not have to embody a Eurocentric thought process. Emergence is the critical phase that drives essential growth.

ACKNOWLEDGMENT

Acknowledgment is the overtly conscious acceptance of one's emerging self with a commitment to develop comfort with emerging views, attitudes, and behaviors. The acknowledgment phase is the most overtly parallel paradigm process within the person, because acknowledgment is not a discount of how one has acted or felt historically; rather, it is a parallel path being explored with full understanding and acceptance of one's current reality.

Acknowledgment is the personal acceptance and exclamation of who one is in spite of the views and attitudes of others. It is the African-American who selects his own labels (in the classic paradigm) rather than letting others label. In the 1960s, it was the Negro selecting "Black"; the Latin male exclaiming himself as "Chicano"; it was the homosexual exclaiming himself as "gay"; the Eurocentric male exclaiming himself as a "feeling man" in spite of societal pressures to not show emotions. It was women claiming themselves as "equal beings entitled to all the benefits achieved by men." Each acknowledgment was and continues to be an intensely personal, and often private, process.

Acknowledgment can be the professional determining that personal and professional decisions will be accomplished through an adherence to personal values—irrespective of the political processes that exist within organizations—even to the realization that it could cost one a job. Acknowledgment is the development of internal influence and power on the self to the exclusion of others' perspectives.

Acknowledgment is the state that Malcom X, Martin Luther King, Jr., Robert Kennedy, Medgar Evers, and other leaders during the Civil Rights era experienced when they recognized that they could be assassinated for their views, and yet chose to move forward with the path that made sense for them. Acknowledgment is a woman exclaiming that she will come forward with a situation of rape in spite of society's treatment of her. Acknowledgment is a whistle blower within an organization whose principles guide the choice to make others aware of the impact of organizational decisions that are unethical or harmful to the public good. Acknowledgment is the ultimate exclamation of desire for congruence with the self.

DISCLOSURE

Disclosure is the public exclamation of the acknowledgment phase of the human development process. When one discloses, one must accept the consequences of the choice to exclaim. Often, people will develop only to the acknowledgment phase and skip the disclosure phase, because internal fears are too great for the projected costs associated with the disclosure.

Disclosure is no longer a private affair that builds on internal strength, but is the active seeking of others with similar views and perspectives to build personal partnerships that ensure survivability with a new perspective or view. Joining the Boy Scouts, the military, the basketball or football team, a gang, or a fraternity or sorority represent milestones people make as personal choices to build on their own perspectives with likeminded persons.

Disclosure becomes the recognition that clinical dysfunction may not be a reality surrounding one's personal view. However, there can be problems with the disclosure. Unions that develop and seek members often force members to acquiesce to the view of the union to the detriment of the individual. This becomes unhealthy disclosure, as being a member of management where participation in political decisions hurts others is seen as unhealthy fracturing of the person and the group. There are so many examples of unhealthy and healthy disclosure, therefore suggesting the critical nature of the disclosure process.

Each of us is accountable for our actions and thoughts in the disclosure process. When we choose to include or find others, we must take responsibility for the impact of the intents we choose to implement. Too often, people want to change or grow within their lives, yet abdicate responsibility for actions that occur as a result of change. Therefore, the disclosure phase is constantly impacted by the acknowledgment and emergence phases. There is a constant reminder of the rationales that have driven personal choices. The more one abdicates, the more the issues of discord begin to creep into the decision-making processes of the individual.

SELF-INDULGENCE

This is a critical, and perhaps the most common, phase of the personal developmental process paradigm. The self-indulgence phase of the paradigm is the pivotal nexus point of the system, for it is the resting place for personal development.

Consider a young gay male discovering himself. He has worked hard to emerge, disclose, and acknowledge himself. He has joined gay and lesbian organizations, works for the change of laws through these organizations, and senses that he is a whole and congruent person. However, he also spends his energies being sexually promiscuous with multiple partners, without looking at the potential of ultimate union with another. Over time, he hurts others in this phase because he manipulates the feelings and desires of others to achieve his sexual interests. He is self-indulgent and harmful of others.

Consider a married man who has worked diligently to develop a wonderful relationship with his wife, yet finds that he is unwilling to help her with responsibilities around the home, exclaiming that it is women's work. He castigates his wife for wanting help or assistance since he is the breadwinner of the home. He has adopted a self-indulgent life posture and is stuck in the developmental process because of views that are inconsistent with the rest of his developmental path.

The self-indulgent phase occurs for people professionally when their actions are designed for self, to the detriment of others. Consider this example of Joseph, a chief executive officer (CEO) of a family foundation. Joseph brings to his foundation an outstanding professional instructor for his program to enhance the academic potential of disadvantaged children. He continually promises Dale, the professional instructor, a contract for services rendered, yet avoids the consummation of the contractual process for self-purposes. The continual denial and discount of Dale is an example of self-indulgent behavior that detrimentally impacts Dale's trust in the relationship. Consequently, Dale finds himself becoming self-conscious in his relationships with others because of the uncertainty exhibited by Joseph. Dale asks himself, "Are all CEOs like Joseph? Can I trust the word of people or must I always test their commitment and honesty?" These examples of self-indulgence block the potential for movement.

Self-indulgence has a "brother" relationship with self-experimentation. The self-experimentation phase in the self-indulgent process is a testing ground for confident and effective choice—or a testing ground for expansions of the self-indulgent, "me-oriented" process. The more the experimentation focuses on healthy choice and movement, the more the person moves to the next phase of re-emergence. The more the experimentation phase leads to expanded me-orientation, the less ready the individual is for movement to a higher phase. Rather, the person revisits discord, emergence, and acknowledgment. Less disclosure occurs because there is internal deceit in the developmental process. The more deceit, the more discord.

RE-EMERGENCE

Re-emergence is the revisiting of existing behavior and value alignment with the historical behavior and value development. People often give up old behaviors and values as they discover and move through new thoughts and actions. It is like a child discovering beer or sex for the first time. Rather than listen to thoughts shared throughout time from the parents, the child explores on his own—often to the discarding of existing family values.

Re-emergence is the rekindling of history with the present and future to build a balanced framework that maintains what is valuable and good about history with what is fluid and good about the present and the future. It is a psychological bonding of the historical life with the new life, filled with a wonderment about what is key to keep and what is a realistic discarding of trappings that do not match or fit with the continually emerging self.

Joyce is the director of the office of management and budget in a computer conglomerate in northern California. Over the past year, she has gotten a divorce from her husband and has been promoted twice in the firm. She has taken on behaviors to reach the top that she is not proud of. She has undercut managers and sold employees down the drain, but has experienced a self-indulgent process that has a positive payoff professionally and financially. What she lost was the sensitivity which originally helped her become the "darling manager" of the corporation. Joyce wanted pieces of her old self back. She liked the influence and power of her new role, and she believed she had a lot to offer the company, but she was not sure who she was any longer.

In the re-emergence, Joyce revisited the discords, emergence, acknowledgments, and disclosures of her emerging self. She explored with a therapist the self-indulgent behaviors she had adopted. Drinking, power manipulations, and compartmentalizing of communications and information had become the norm for her. She did not like what she had become and wanted to change again. The re-emergence stage allows one to rethink their development and revisit and alter that development to a pattern that seems to retain and expand on underlying values that guide overall action. When we emerge and change, we may not always bring with us the values that are essential to our total being. We may embrace values that move us through acknowledgment and disclosure but be somewhat out of sync with what is really important to us. As we review and revisit, we often find pieces of our history that expand us as open systems, that nurture us as beings in the society, and that frame for us the whole that is critical to lasting comfort.

Re-emergence then becomes the conscious in our development. It defines the sense of living spirit that allows us to meet the world head-on and frame a true niche that works for who we are more so than what we do. In effect, re-emergence helps us frame the balance that is necessary for continued development.

CONGRUENCE

Congruence is the development of the systems path within the human being. Issues of premises, assumptions, cultural transitions, professional and personal roles, behavior, communication, protocol, and etiquette are all drivers in blending what one experiences in the other phases to this phase. It is not a static phase, but it is a more structured frame for balancing action with thought, personal with professional, values with assumptions, and current reality with personal history.

In the congruence process, values and how one accommodates, negotiates, bridges one space to another, and creates new norms become most important. One's history—whether ethnic (race), economic (rich or poor), biological (male or female), ontological (young or old), familial (large or small family), relational (single or in a union), or psychological/cultural (gay or straight, domestic or foreign)—impacts one's ability to be congruent. All parts of history are blended with emerging values and attitudes that may have changed one's perspective in any or all of the aforementioned categories.

Dinah Shore, the television actress, once said that the recognition that she was African-American versus Caucasian significantly altered her reality of the world and how the world responded to her. She felt that she had coasted through life without thought to who she was or what was important. The realization of an ethnic change altered her realities in every dimension. Discord became her norm, and only through processing her life and needs was she able to rebuild a congruent life that meant something to her. Only through this was she able to impact differently the realities that others wanted to create.

Each of us goes through a developmental process where ups and downs frame our thinking. We analyze, we accept, we avoid, we cajole, we move forward. However, somewhere in the process, we look for the congruity of the life and strive to make sense of what is. The making sense is the challenge of congruence. We challenge ourselves ultimately when we risk growing and developing from a process perspective rather than from a compartmentalized and fragmented approach to our development. Generalizations, abstractions, techniques, and xenophobic perspectives leave; and we are left with the nakedness of who we are and how we have come to a point in time.

Congruence is the vigilant and constant movement in the process paradigm. People process in an intentional manner to ensure that all the parts make a larger whole.

THE IMPACTS OF A PROCESS PARADIGM APPROACH

Business is currently trapped in an analytical thinking approach to development of long-term strategies for the implementation and management of business. The analytical thinking approach feeds the process of compartmentalization, fragmentation, and detachment that haunts successful business venturing. In this approach, focus on control, structure, individual performance, semi-teams, power, directed approach, and other fractured terms become the norm for the assessment and implementation of new strategies. The failure of the fragmented functions is the inability to craft solutions to issues that cause businesses to succeed or fail.

Businesses succeed because they can embrace new issues and craft different solutions from the past. Systems-oriented terminology includes words such as collaboration, cooperation, teamwork, partnerships, alliances, self-directed teams, self-regulated teams, process-oriented teams, process-oriented strategies, and open-system strategies. Support systems and operating systems bridge history to craft parallel strategies for the resolution of business issues to achieve realistic business outcomes.

Look at any business organization. Support functions of human resources, finance, legal, and public relations are critical to the overall success of the business venture. Operating areas of research, production, sales, and marketing are driven by the support departments. Windows 95 is an excellent example of the challenges of the two parts of a whole. Marketing and research identified a critical delivery date to the public. Research, production, and project teams drove the delivery process; however, the effectiveness of the structure was based on the ability of human resources to hire and retain competent personnel, legal to identify and resolve critical issues of patents to the technology being employed, finance to agree to the expenditure of resources for the product development and marketing, and public relations to maintain the high trust of the public. The product was released on time; however, the effectiveness of the software was moderate in comparison to other releases from Microsoft. All the right things had been in place—strategic plans, business plans, individual plans, and goals—yet it was not totally successful. What happened to all the issues required in a business process paradigm? Did the release of the product ensure that the quality of the product development process would mirror the history of the company? Were there misinterpretations of the roles and policies that guide overall quality testing and quality delivery? Commitment seemed to be clearly in focus. However, did commitment overshadow reciprocity in the development, marketing, and sales processes? Did finance drive the actions of the firm, or did the product? Where was representation and empowerment in the process? Did the organization allow equality in ensuring that the separate components of the business decision were connected to the purpose of the product? Empowerment seemed to have been in place in the training and development of the employees to provide assistance to the customers, but were the elements, boundaries, causes, and qualities essential to an effective system in place? Did the process drive the development of Windows 95 or did the release of a new product drive the system? The fact that numerous issues are arising suggests the latter.

So what can the process paradigm generate that closed-end analytical paradigms seem to overlook? First is the empowering of individuals to move toward self-mastery. There is a need within the human being to improve personal competency and effectiveness. The self-mastery process sets the stage for the individual to improve interpersonal and working relationships and the effectiveness of all persons on the team. The concept of excellence has meaning when people experience representation and empowerment. Second, intergroup relations are enhanced in such a fashion that business processes between teams and departments horizontally are enhanced, thereby increasing the quality of customer service. Third, the total organization begins to experience a better fit than has been a part of its history. Systems, structures, and processes flow together because there is a commitment to the process more than the product. The commitment to process guides the product development and delivery. Last, the environment surrounding the organization is enhanced because business leaders and business members—as well as the employees—understand the direction and process of the organization.

The business process paradigm and the human process paradigm set the stage for organizational leaders and the organizational system to truly embrace the strategic process. Discussions of the future state drive the feedback-loop process that assesses the current state. With some understanding of these issues, the organization can begin to focus on the critical issue of the transition state. The balance of all the issues creates a greater whole than has previously been experienced by the organization.

Vision, mission, customer focus, quality, service, environmental cost, profitability, stakeholder focus, and society become part of the future state. Critical values regarding how the future state is to be achieved become essential issues for the future state discussion. Teamwork, self-directed teams, process teams, employee empowerment, total quality management, quality-improvement process, and communication strategies are all a part of the future state discussion because they help frame the process of equality, interpretation, reciprocity, empowerment, and commitment of the business process paradigm. Remember, it is the *process* that guides, not the *product*.

The feedback process looks at success and weakness. What has worked? What has been less than successful? Did we benchmark and develop strategies for defining and framing success? Did we assess the effectiveness of what has gone before us? Is there any research that guides? Was the research analytically focused, or was the research an appreciative inquiry process that mirrored an open system? If the research was achieved through a closed-end analytical process, then it is probably the wrong information, thus requiring that we use an appreciative-inquiry process to develop information for strategy development.

Did we look at the current state? Was there any information from current processes that could be beneficial in the future state? How did we address the compartmentalized and fragmented areas of service management, quality service, speed and response time, business processes, sales, marketing, costs, culture change based on product development, structure, and support systems? Did we do the analysis in a vacuum? If so, maybe analytical thinking is not the approach. Instead, systems analysis from an open systems assessment may give us better and more useful information.

THE NATURE OF SYSTEMS AND THE IMPORTANCE OF CHANGING

Organizations as systems can not be understood in compartmentalized and fragmented ways: Systems can only be understood from a holistic framework. Elements, cause, boundaries, qualities, and relations are all parts of a system and can only be fully understood when they are viewed as a whole; therefore, it is important to look at them as a whole. If you change any component of a system, the whole system is affected and therefore the entire system must be addressed. When you focus exclusively on one element of a system without equal attention to the other elements of the system, the system fails.

Table 7.4 depicts the difference between analytical thinking and systems thinking. You will notice that the analytical thinking process is very self-directed and perpetuates the dysfunctions, disconnects, and

Table 7.4
The Duality of Analytical and Systems Thinking

Analytical Thinking	Systems Thinking
Opposites - We versus They	Partners - Employees, Customers
Independent Focus	Interdependent Focus
Activities and Tasks	Outcomes
Problem Resolution	Shared Vision Guiding Action
Work Groups and Departments	Total Organization
Specific Skill Base	Cross-Functional Work Teams
Department Missions and Goals	Core Values, Core Strategies
Hierarchical Structure	Open Space Cyclical Teams
Individualistic and Singular Change	Systems Change

frustrations of the corporate America. If we are to survive societally and organizationally, then a shift in the paradigms that guide our functioning becomes more critical than ever.

Organizations must become open systems if they are to survive. Therefore, organizations only work when there is mutual interaction with the internal changes of people and actions *and* when there is interaction with the changing environment that molds the people within the system. Ultimately, no system can be understood by analysis—systems can only be understood by synthesis of the process of assessing the whole of the system.

LEADING AND CHANGING FOR THE FUTURE

CHAPTER

8

Using the Parallel Paradigms to Make Choices

We have been traveling a path to changing the choices that we make in the business environment. The choices are framed in an open space, open systems paradigm, rather than the traditional closed systems analytical paradigms. The factors that guide choices often have underlying values that either override the potential of systems to be effective or enhance the overall potential of systems to engage and embrace the wholeness of a society in the development of products and processes. Elements of the new paradigms were discussed in Chapter 7, yet we have not talked of the overarching uses of the paradigms. This chapter focuses on the overall impacts of the paradigms and the choices it causes leaders and members of an organization or family to embrace.

OPEN SYSTEMS/CLOSED SYSTEMS: PERSPECTIVES ON BUSINESS AND PEOPLE

The organizational and personal challenge that comes from this book is based on the parallel paradigms of Chapter 7. For years, businesses and people have followed the paradigms of cause and effect or evolution without balancing what occurs for the person and the business in concert with one another. Yet the reality of business and people development is that they are not totally separate entities. People develop and change based on the environmental experiences they have with business. Businesses change because of the environmental and interactive

experiences they have with people. What usually has not been effectively understood or assessed is the efficacy of the systems that are in
place surrounding the interactions of people and business.

Strategically, Chapter 7 addressed issues of development and movement within organizations and among people through a process paradigm. Sometimes, however, executives and employees would read that
dialogue on process paradigms and state that their current organizational
structure or their current rules were in sync with that perspective, yet miss
the points that are critical to the overall understanding of the issue.

We are talking about both the change of a system and the compre-
hensiveness of the system. Two thoughts guide the overall nature of that
discussion. Is your business a closed or open business system? Do your
employees operate best in a closed business system, or would your employees operate more effectively in an open business system?

Closed Business Systems

Closed business systems are focused on clear, identifiable goal attainment. Traditionally, the process of goal attainment focuses on the estab-
lishment of rules and procedures that govern the potential of the
organization to achieve the identified goal and, in so doing, increase
the potential of the organization to operate and view itself in a rational
manner. Goals and purpose are explicit in this system, and attention is
focused on maintaining that clarity in a rational explanation of what is
right rather than what is possible.

Decisions within a closed system are based on the legitimate and established rules and procedures that have guided organizational action.
If decisions that confront one are outside the established rules or one's
role within the organization, then the decision must be pushed upward
to maintain the rationality of the system. You can see that boundaries
are tight. If the decision is wrong, then punishment is the clear outcome for the person in the system, because the wrong decision makes
it impossible for the organization to remain rational.

Most of society operates from a closed system model. Contracts, compensation, promotion, and retention are based on the ability of the
organization and its members to maintain a rational approach to business, and if creativity is a part of the system process, it is addressed in
the ability of a rational model to respond to issues of complexity, specialization, and training to maintain the rational mind. Organizations
look at the changes that confront them and determine that it will meet
the challenge through more training, more specialty-skilled employees,
or through structural options to address complexity. In this process, the
appearance to employees is that the organization is caring and concerned about employee development. To the contrary, the organization

is concerned with the ability of the organization to continue to maintain control and stay focused on a predetermined end. True cause and effect is the outcome of the closed systems model. The dissonance is based on the understanding that society is not always rational, and thus a tension between organizations, people, and societal spirit is always present.

Open Business Systems

Open systems have been called natural systems. While open systems consider the goal issues of the organization, they also recognize the goals of the organization as only one component of a comprehensive system. The underlying basis of an open system is the concept of development or change and how the organization responds to the changes rather than reacts to the changes. Issues of strategies, environment, diversity, community, and "quirks" all impact the open system as unplanned factors. Katz and Kahn, in *Social Psychology of Organizations*, state that there are nine characteristics of open systems that are critical for organizations:

1. The importance of organizational and personal energy. Energy is generated within the organization every time new people are brought into the organization.

2. The process of work is a critical open system concept. How one accomplishes the issues of the organization is essential to open systems.

3. The output of the organization is a critical component of the open system. No matter what emerges from the work of the employees, all of the outputs of the organization are utilized to achieve full utilization of the organization's products.

4. The energetic use of systems energy feeds the development of critical subsystems that can change over time. The more the organization reflects on its use of energy given to the system, the more the organization alters itself to be responsive.

5. The concept of negative entropy is important. Businesses often bring more energy into the system than it can handle. Inventory stockpiling becomes an important component of the open system.

6. Management of information is critical so that the organization does not become overloaded and unable to process data that helps in decision making and organizational change.

7. There are basic systems that remain, regardless of the changes around the system.

8. Differentiation is a critical business concept in open systems. How the organization embraces changes and elaborations of roles and accountabilities within the organization is important. How the organization maximizes skills and abilities to craft new specialities is important.

9. Equifinality is the base line strategy of open systems. How the organization brings multiple strategies to get to the same outcomes is critical.

Organizations are impacted by the energies and inputs that come from the environment and the society, and the organization is intentional in embracing the inputs to guide the short and long term.

THE STRUCTURE OF LIVING BUSINESS: HOW PARADIGMS CAN GUIDE

Three critical concerns have always come to my mind as I have thought of the concept of business. Every business has a philosophy, a spirit, and a psychological framework. My impressions of today's businesses become frustrating because of the lack of clear presence of a philosophy, spirit, and psychological framework. Business is framed by these three critical perspectives, and without the perspectives, businesses follow a set pattern of life that ultimately ends. I am not sure that I believe that any business has to end. In fact, I sense that any business can live forever if it is clear about its wholeness and the congruence of its members.

BUSINESS PHILOSOPHY: THE OPEN SYSTEMS CHOICE

The open systems choice focuses on changing the paradigms that people and businesses utilize to make choices that impact the lives of organizations and the members who make the organization function. The critical issue in the open systems process is the reevaluation of the underlying assumptions that guide business decision making.

One of the underlying assumptions is that the structure of an organization should mirror the social structures that have created personal and family development. When each of us developed, we found comfort in the hierarchical structure of the family: father and mother as authority figures, siblings as peers to assist in shouldering the responsibility, grandparents as the leaders of the family system, and aunts and uncles as teachers and supporters of the system in place. There was a measure of control attached to the system, and control allowed us to develop without too much harm and too many tangential movements away from the structure.

As we grew older, we took the family system for granted, yet we understood its place in our lives. Organizations have traditionally utilized the same structure in crafting authority models for corporate action. This structure within organizations establishes order, rules, and punishments for violations of existing rules. Employees may not always like the rules, just as they often did not like the rules within the family; yet they followed the rules by and large because they provided some measure of comfort.

The second assumption is that a closed-end system enhances the images of people and systems in its ability to establish the anchors that people and systems need to operate effectively. This assumption is a difficult one to handle, as it is based on the belief that people and systems cannot operate freely and must be contained. The impact of the assumption is that fear usually governs the actions of people and political actions within organizations. Therefore, no person and no rule can ultimately be valued. Control and power become the true regulators of behavior and thought. Thus the concept of trust is an anathema to personal and organizational development.

The third assumption is that a sense of community is always more important than the individual. This requires that individuation takes a back seat to the needs of the community, and that the group's thinking is more important than individual thought or action. What is good for one is good for all. Treating each employee in a special way is unacceptable, thus requiring that all employees be treated the same, even when that creates more problems than are necessary.

The concept of open systems challenges all of the assumptions heretofore mentioned and frees the human and business spirit to assess and evaluate the efficacy of the assumptions. In effect, open systems allow each person and each organization to evaluate (1) ways of being—the psychological business process; (2) ways of knowing—the spiritual business process; and (3) ways of behaving—the theoretical and technical business processes. When you challenge the assumptions that have guided one's decisions, you free the decision-making process to be special for each and every issue or action. This is a very critical issue for the development of organizations and the development of people. There is no magical method that must exist for business development, decisions, and success. The process of looking at each issue through the process paradigms frees the organization and the person to be truly present and authentic in the impacts of the decision. This becomes helpful because it releases the system to function on issues, not personalities. This release allows the decision makers to address organizational culture, structures, groups, and individuals as both separate entities and a part of the comprehensive whole. The challenging of assumptions becomes the freeing process. The hard part in the process is developing a systematic way of assessment and evaluation.

Movement through Transformation

Jack Mezirow wrote about Jergen Habermas in *Transformative Dimensions of Adult Learning*, stating "What we [society or leaders] have perfected is instrumental learning, the capacity to solve specific discrete technical problems in the world through the application of the scientific method of analysis and implementation. What we have devalued and ignored are the capacities implied by communicative learning, the domain in which we learn to discover and develop values, find ways to resolve conflicts and manage complexity." In his book, Mezirow also speaks of emancipatory learning. Emancipatory learning is the domain where discovery of perception and action occur. The freedom in the discovery is based on the extent of communicative learning possible. Our process of knowing or learning is often based on different strategies that allow approaching one another to explore new thoughts, new issues, and new beliefs. Our learning must become an integrated process of dialoguing between all parties impacted by the issues. Technical resolution is a compartmentalized resolution. Communicative learning and emancipatory learning become the methods for a comprehensive resolution strategy for business decision making and ultimate business action. This process is called transformative learning.

When I first heard of transformative learning, I was struck by the words transform, learn, emancipate, and communicate. I began to think of the business environments in which I have watched and participated in decision making. None of those terms were ever used. None of those terms ever crept into the halls of the ivory towers of business. None of the employees spoke of learning, transforming, freeing, or communicating. All spoke of power, control, limits, boundaries, and restrictions, and the decisions rendered met the tests of the latter words. Decisions were controlling, limiting, binding, and restricting. There was influence in the words spoken by Mezirow, and the words reminded me of Gibb and Venerable as I looked at these concepts three years ago. There was potential to move my clients farther than ever before, because there were possibilities for the paradigms to change.

So what is this transformative process? Transformation is the restructuring or altering of beliefs and values based on a reevaluation of the underlying assumptions that guide thought, action, and being. Imagine altering business beliefs because you reassessed the meaning of the assumptions that had always guided your decision making. Imagine your employees altering their beliefs about business, management, unions, and self, because the underlying assumptions surrounding personhood, culture, socialization (and society), and learning were challenged. This could become a different business world. I believe it is becoming a different business world because the old paradigms have ceased to work. The old paradigms have restricted creation, and the old paradigms have caused dysfunctions that block growth and development.

The Value of Thought: Changing Our Thinking for the Present and Future

My friends have always said that I think too much. My associates and the business organizations in which I have worked have always said that my focus on "the right thing to do" takes too long and seems to miss the point, because it requires a long, slow process to get at an appropriate answer. I find that parallel process paradigms and critically assessing underlying assumptions become the only rational and emotional strategies to resolving issues and developing systems and people. We change and grow because we take the time to be present—to be all there—in the assessment and development of solutions to business and personal action. The more we become cognizant of all the factors and issues, the more likely we are to create comprehensive, congruent, and whole responses to the issues of business and people.

Thinking is the key to congruent and holistic development and success. The process of inquisitive and comprehensive thinking focuses on a pattern of questioning that empowers communicative and emancipatory learning to occur as an avenue to address issues and frame possibilities inherent in the questions postulated for business and personal action. These processes look at the context and content of the conversations and dynamics of the issues. *Context* is the framework in which the issues are raised. Each and every time an issue or discussion occurs, a context for that discussion or issue exists that frames how the issue should be viewed. *Content* is the "meat and potatoes" of the discussion. The subject and the particulars surrounding any given topic frame the content of any issue. Numerous strategies exist for critical analysis discussions surrounding issues. An easy one that allows one to effectively address a comprehensive approach to thinking is the following:

1. Be clear about the issue or subject to be discussed and understood. Define the parameters that are critical to the discussion. Ask, "Is it a clarification process, or is it a change process?"

2. Gather enough data to clearly describe the issue at hand. What has occurred that causes the issue to be of primary importance at this point in time? When did the phenomenon occur? Was it a one-time situation, or has it been occurring over a longer period of time? Were there contributing circumstances that caused it to exist? Is it a long-standing issue that has been avoided over time?

3. Are there underlying assumptions that have guided the analysis of the situation, or are the assumptions allowing one to miss critical analysis points because of the assumptions in play?

4. Assess your congruence with the underlying assumptions. If you discover that the underlying assumption is still the critical dynamic in the discussion and analysis, keep the assumption and review other criteria for assessment. If you discover that the assumption no longer applies to the content and context, change it to more accurately reflect the issue.

5. Revisit the context and the content that now causes a change in the underlying assumptions. Remember, it is the assumption that is at issue, not the content or context. If the context is skewed, then assess what is required to alter it to more accurately reflect the needs of the organization and/or the person or group.

6. Revisit the value of the issue—the context and content. Often when the assumptions change, the context and content are no longer important in the transformative process.

7. If change is required, then remember key concepts that guide the change process. If the context is not correct, reframe it to fit the parameters in question. If the content or the particulars are not accurate, replace it with more appropriate data that allow an accurate balance with the underlying assumptions. If both the context and content are not correct, then strategize avenues to blend the two in manners that create a synergy between them. This is critical to ensure that tandem working occurs.

The Value of the Communication Process

Organizations, with their size, technology, and complexity, evolve into information systems. Whenever an organization is created or structured, there is a belief that the organization will move down a predetermined path that frames communication within itself. Decision making, leadership, influence, and power all need and require the communication process to ensure outcomes that maintain the organization. The communication process within organizations should ensure the accuracy of information, the appropriate emotive boundaries for all the members of the organization, and the appropriate spiritual and living spirit of the business for all the members of the organization. It should display the theoretical and practical boundaries that guide all organizational action. The communication process is, by action and definition, a relational process. One person sends information, and the other receives it. The interpretation of the message becomes critical to the clarity of the information sent and received. This is the process of business and the process of relationship building. When the communication process is unclear or garbled, then the effectiveness of the organization (and the effectiveness of the relationships within the business) falters, and the potential for ineffective assessment of issues and the context and content of the issues gets lost. Business and its members therefore must address the communication process as an essential underlying assumption for success.

IMPACTS OF THE UNDERLYING ASSUMPTIONS ON OPEN SYSTEMS

Underlying Assumptions

When one operates from a closed system, the membranes of the paradigm tightly frame what is allowable in the relationships and experiences of the members of the organization. Primary in that process is the cause-and-effect paradigm thinking. There must be some reason, some action, some blame for the changes to the system. The impact is the creation of organizational violence among the members of the system. This means that issues of self, issues of groups, and issues of community are stifled in the developmental process of the business. The rules and norms of the organization are already framed, and the potential of the members of the organization to impact the success of the organization has been stifled into nonexistence.

Open systems, therefore, free the organization to utilize the gifts and talents of the members and the system to create change, assess issues, and alter the context and content to address external and internal development. Jack Gibb postulated that "only through the freeing of people and systems can the system begin to meet its value to the society and the community. Tightly structuring the organization, controlling all the decisions, hampering the development and diversity of the members of an organization create dysfunctions that destroy the system and its members."

Historical Behavior

Closed systems are historical systems. What has gone before establishes the framework for what can occur in the future. In the closed systems process, hiring of managers is based on the ability of the manager to fit with the history of the organization more than the ability to get the work accomplished. In the closed systems process, change is always incremental and, therefore, ineffective because the history of the organization— how things have always been—drives the process of change. In a closed system, the concept of inclusion and diversity become anathemas to the system because history focuses on groupthink, not diversity.

History is not all bad, yet history does impede the clean assessment of issues within organizations. Consider a fire department or police department where employees survive within the system based on entitlement—how long they have been with the organization. A new employee comes on board with differing ideas for responding to the mission of the organization. History—how things have always been accomplished—impedes the ability of the organization to embrace new concepts and ideas. History closes the potential of the organization to understand new content and contexts.

Consider a new CEO who has been hired from a different corporation. The CEO wants to establish new methods for accomplishing work. As time marches on, the analytical historical assessment by the members of the organization sets in motion strategies to block the changes because it violates the history of the organization. Over time, the CEO finds that thought and action to change to a new organizational paradigm are thwarted and the communication issues around power take over and destroy the potential for change. History is the culprit.

Open systems allow movement away from historical modeling. Traditional strategies for analysis and decision making can be challenged and altered because the underlying assumptions that guided the context and content can be assessed and changed. Open systems confront the concept of self and group and often create new contexts for identifying and understanding the issues of self and group. This movement allows an expansion of organizations and people to address the critical need for community in the business development.

Homogenous People Systems

I have always been struck by the concept of "fit" in human resource management decision making in the selection and promotion process of employees. Organizational leaders seem to want comfort more than performance, and craft elaborate strategies for justifying homogeneity. Closed systems focus on exclusion and sameness. The entrepreneurial process that created organizations and allowed the development of conglomerates gets destroyed by the inability of the organization to diversify and broaden its boundaries to attract and reflect the community of customers critical to success.

Organizations in 1990 America operate from the concept of fit. That does not mean that there are not attempts to diversify and include; rather, it means that attempts to embrace diversity and live with discomfort is a very small component of organizational life. There is a belief that the thought processes for success in business must come from the same paradigm thinking parameters. White corporate executives are comfortable with persons who "think as they think" and have similar experiences. Persons of color are set up to fail in that system. Maintaining an Afrocentric thinking process or a First American paradigm will cause problems for the person of color and discomfort for the person of Eurocentric thought.

Open systems thinking therefore provides a freshness and a movement away from single-loop learning. Double-loop learning, multiple-paradigm thinking, and diversity-inclusion processes are strategies for expanding what you have always experienced to a different context with expanded content. This is a critical change for business because it recognizes that history does not mean present and future; rather, history only represents a baseline for starting to expand who one is, what one does, and how one grows.

This is a critical concept for the future. All the data sets over the past fifteen years have focused on the changing demographics of business. The demographics suggest that different systems thinking models will inevitably be present in business because persons of color and women will be the majority in the workforce. This change over time suggests that business must prepare itself in the communication and dialogue processes by challenging its own paradigms. As an example, consider myself. I am an African-American professor of business in a university committed to diversity inclusion by its mission and its constant report. Yet it is often interesting for me to sense professors and administrators of this university react to thoughts from myself or other persons of color from paradigms that restrict and block opportunity for growth and change. This is not an intentional blockage, but rather a blockage based on using historical and homogenous thought for evaluation. The same is true in the business corporations of America. Intentionality is not always the issue, just history and homogeneity. This is important for the persons of color and women to remember, for it reduces the need to embrace all frustration from an emotive and personal perspective.

Identifying the system and paradigms in operation can be liberating, allowing one to craft new strategies to help the organization and its members make movement. Not everything is personal, intentional, or planned—often things just happen—but the critical thinking process of assessment becomes a critical part of the learning paradigm and the change process.

Movement from Self to Community

The most difficult component of closed systems is the focus on self. Closed systems perpetuate a preoccupation with the self. When one focuses on the closed system paradigm, preoccupation with the context of self is prevalent—based on the control processes that are primary in the closed paradigm process. When control is the ultimate outcome of the system, protection and self-directed activity is essential to overall survival. Remember that control establishes restrictions and fear, therefore forcing one to focus on internal protective energies versus collaborative and expansive strategies for implementations of business options and relational practices.

The open systems paradigm frees the individual to move beyond a myopic approach to business and personal development. The open systems paradigm focuses on liberation and expansion. There is opportunity for exploring the consciousness of the person and the community rather than retreating into the unconscious as a strategy for protection.

You might ask, "How is this an advantage for business?" Businesses ultimately thrive on the potential of the organization to effectively bond with the community. Strategies that empower employees to create new contexts and contents free the community to experience the passion and care for the continued valuing of the community. With a closed system, community is a thought in the wind or a strategy for maintenance of the system. Open systems establish a spiritual connection with community that advances the relational constructs of complete joining and sharing. This thought was originally postulated by the theologian, Martin Buber (1923). Buber stated that man seeks absolute harmony and understanding with a higher power in order to expand what he has been in his past with what he can become in his present and future. Businesses seek that same I–Thou experience in order to move beyond finite possibilities to infinite changes for the present and future. When the preoccupation is on the self, the experiences are only I–It experiences. Some translation of the value of community becomes lost.

Open systems establish real credible strategies for organizational and personal movement. Only through an open process can exploration, understanding, transformation, and liberation be attained by organizations and systems.

THE PROCESS OF TRANSFORMING BUSINESS

Businesses are continually looking for strategies to alter current actions to enhance the overall market and profit margins. Businesses have employed technological strategies to move them from one place in history to another. The impact of these strategies has often been the annihilation of the human condition and the extrication of true strategies that transform the business to a dimension of excellence and influence.

I sense that the utilization of process paradigms will significantly alter the business systems in operation within business. Closed systems and open systems have their limitation in the long-term impact of control and power. I believe that the more organizations focus on the parallel process paradigms, the more they will recognize that open space is critical to business survivability; yet there is a need for businesses and people to reframe the nature of production and process to craft a new perspective for business delivery. The answer may truly be in the developmental models of people, not in the developmental process of business.

In Chapters 9 and 10, we look at the impact of transforming business by changing the context and the content of business action and business thinking. Suffice it to say, businesses must begin to become learning communities that develop comprehensive strategies for long-term business decision making and people development. This process embodies the development of competencies that focus on evolution and inclusion, expansion and exploration, and congruence and wholeness.

CHAPTER 9

TRANSFORMING BUSINESS, TRANSFORMING EMPLOYEES

The Development of
Competencies That Expand,
Empower, and Explore: The Trinity
Process of Business and Personal
Development

In Chapters 7 and 8, we explored the development of parallel paradigms that are process based with no end, and we have explored the critical nature of open systems versus closed systems in the business and personal realm. This chapter focuses on essential competencies that enhance the potential of people and systems to effectively interact and craft context and content for business development. These areas are a tripartate system of competencies that coalesce and blend three dimensions of business and human development. The tripartate system involves (1) human/psychological competency development, (2) theoretical/ philosophical competency development, and (3) spiritual- and value-based competency development.

THE TRINITY: SPIRIT, HUMANITY, AND CONTEXT

When I think about business leaders, I am often torn with the struggles they have in developing long-term strategies for ensuring overall business success versus the lack of options they seem to understand or employ to effectively make changes for the future. Linear and dualistic thought often seem to be the strategies of the theorists and the practitioners that get displayed for business leaders. This is an exploration of transformation for business and people because it focuses on a three-dimensional approach to business. All three areas are needed for business to incorporate the history of the organization, be it closed or open. All three areas of the tripartite system are needed for people to feel empowered to participate fully in the development and implementation of business.

I call this process, "Trinity: Spirit, Humanity, and Context," because all three represent a wholeness and congruence that is missed by the current business strategies of organizations and their members. Each person brings to the organization an underlying spirit—passions and histories that frame how they operate within the business. Each person has a context for action that is superimposed by a business context that they may or may not understand. As each person has a spirit that pushes and pulls on their behavior, each organization has a context that frames how it looks at the development of people within the organization—framing the roles, responsibilities, accountabilities, and movement of the people and the organization. Each organization has a baseline spirit that has framed how it operates and moves within a community and a humanity (in the family sense) that frames how it embraces or restricts growth, development, conflict, radicalism, passive aggressive or passive dependent behavior, thought, action, and process.

What is unique about this trinity is that there is never a completion, only a continual movement toward congruence and wholeness. People and organizations change, and all of the changes are a part of the trinity. There is no end, only milestones along the way toward organizational living. Survival is not the outcome, living is. Control is not the outcome, collaboration is. Power is not the outcome, influence is. Product is not the outcome, process is.

This is a significantly different approach to understanding business, education, development, and profit. This trinity is about continual transformation and requires a trust and belief that "everything will work out" in the business frame. It involves reframing information to banks for credit information. It requires synergizing with communities to frame new outcomes for the living spirit of the community. It requires the creation of competencies, not products, so that every movement in business is based on the utilization of competencies to respond to environmental and internal influences. It is a process of exploration, not problem solving, for *process* is the strategy, not product.

THE TRINITY SYSTEM PROCESS OF BUSINESS AND PERSONAL DEVELOPMENT

The trinity process is a tripartite system of wholeness and congruence development to personal and business functioning. The structure of the system focuses on collaboration and coalescing of three systems areas that impact and influence business and personal development to achieve continual movement and improvement of people and systems. Three uniquely independent (yet interdependent) strategies work collaboratively to comprehensively approach business and personal development. These are called the context, spirit, and humanity of the business and personal process development.

Figures 9.1 and 9.2 depict the tripartite system. The system addresses three continuous movements, each depicted individually in Figures 9.3, 9.4, and 9.5, on a circular continuum that frames developmental being and action. One portion of the continuum focuses on the context of the trinity. The context of the trinity is made up of the parallel process paradigms

Figure 9.1
The Trinity Process

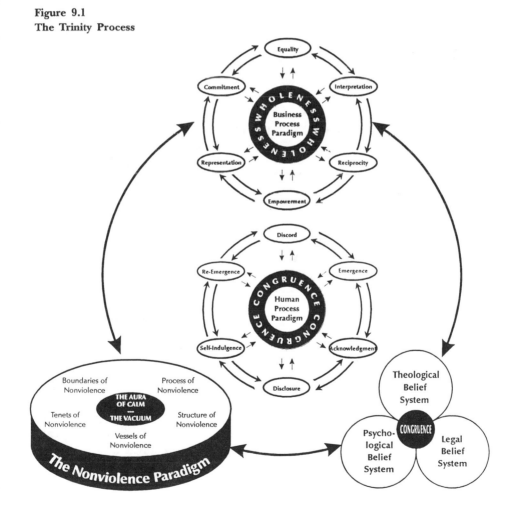

Figure 9.2
The Trinity Process in Motion

that frame how business and people look at the development of business. The spirit of the trinity is the assessment of underlying values and belief systems that impact business and personal choice. The humanity of the trinity focuses on the manner in which people and systems address the personal concerns of organizational members. How the organization addresses dialogue, community, and communion with one another is essential to the congruence of the trinity. Figure 9.6 identifies all the competencies required for wholeness in business and congruence within people. It depicts all the components held by a total system.

To be effective, organizational leaders and the members of the organization initially look at the outcomes that frame entrepreneurship and business action. The outcome of the entrepreneurship is not static; rather, it is an evolutionary process of injecting into society a process that alters the society. Whether it be the production of a new car, new computer, new construction process, or new service initiative, the process is evolutionary. Whether it is the inclusion of diversity, persons of color, persons who are gay or lesbian, or persons from differing cultures, the impact on the organization is evolutionary. Whether it is control-based, power- or authority-based, empowerment- or inclusion-based, or chaos-free–based, the process of emerging business is evolutionary. Evolutionary development is process-based development, so when businesses stop the evolutionary process to craft a closed system, they end the evolutionary process and begin the process of business demise and business death. When people come to an organization because of the excitement and challenge espoused by the system and find themselves in fear of the

Figure 9.3
Context

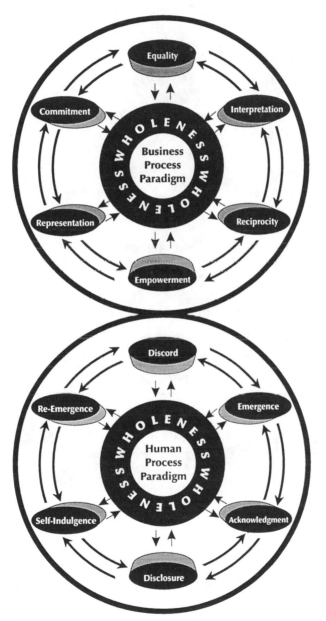

Figure 9.4
Spirit

Figure 9.5
Humanity: The Impact on People and Organizations

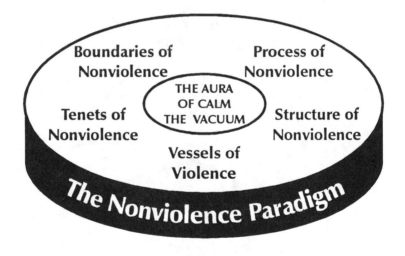

organizational dynamics, the process of personal demise and personal death begins. The loss of evolution, continual creation, humanity, spirit, and context cause a spiraling death for people and systems that is an anathema to the evolutionary ethos.

So what can work in a realistic and practical manner? What can create profits beyond imagination while creating holistic and congruent

Figure 9.6
Competencies for Trinity Process Students

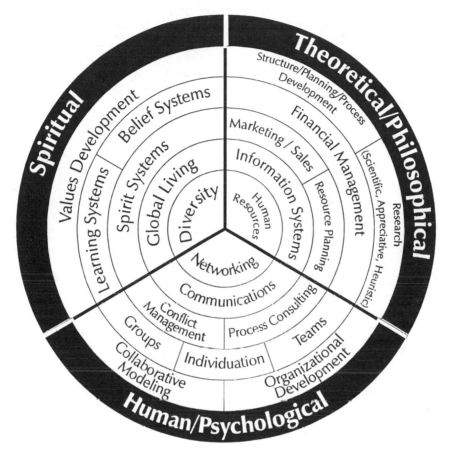

processes and actions? What can drive continual renewal in business and among people? I strongly assert that the trinity process can and does!

THE TRINITY SYSTEM: EXPLORATIONS INTO CONTINUUMS

If you will remember, earlier in this chapter I talked of the tripartate system where the process paradigms frame how business and people look at the development of business. Revisiting Figure 9.3, you see that fluidness is the crux of one part of the trinity. In the process paradigms, there is no beginning or end—only levels of development that flow as changes flow for the person or organization. This is a key component of contiuums. Issues of procedure, function, managing, integrating, renewing, and unity all become essential outcomes of the process paradigms. The person and the organization continually focus on congruity in the decision-making process. There is continual focus on emergence and interpretation of data that feeds change for the person and the organization. There is fluidness in reciprocity and acknowledgment. Each level of understanding creates movement toward congruence and wholeness for the person and the organization. The more one understands self or the system, the more one embraces change that allows differing perspectives in disclosure and empowerment.

There is a continual synergy between the person and the organization, breeding life and spirit into the interactions that govern movement and change. When stasis is occurring in self-indulgence and representation, the pull to move toward congruity and holism forces the person and the organization to embrace the compartmentalization that begins to occur. The challenge of stasis becomes the re-emergence for the person and the reexamination of commitment for the business. Congruence and wholeness become the outcomes of the process for the person and the system.

There is a freshness that comes over an executive or an employee when they recognize that being perfect, having the answer, and making mistakes are all a part of the developmental process. That ease of experience sets the stage for true blending from one part of the system to the other. The developmental paradigms free the person and the organization to include the environment, community, and cultures of numerous persons and organizations to craft a different congruence and a different whole.

SPIRIT: THE VALUES AND BELIEFS
OF THE TRINITY PROCESS

Figure 9.4 focuses on the spirit of the person and organization. The spirit represents the underlying values, assumptions, and beliefs and belief systems that impact business and personal choice.

Values, beliefs, and choices are critical components in our attempts to be consistently functional. Values and beliefs guide our ability to recognize right from wrong, make choices regarding friends, accept positions within companies, or select a significant other. Values and beliefs establish the parameters for our moral fibers, and they create the framework for our flexibility to respond to others whom we perceive as different from ourselves. However, changes in our comfort zones created by economic crises, increased religious pressure, and discomfort with accepting differing values and beliefs have caused the majority to say personally and often in business, "Enough—stop the growing and changing.

Conform to our expectations or be seen as less valuable than we see ourselves." With these constrictions comes dysfunctional behavior that threatens the very fiber of the democratic process. This, in theory, suggests that individuals should be able to carry their opinions, values, and beliefs into practice, as long as they do not infringe upon the rights of others. The fear associated with change and newness often defeats the spirit of organizations and the spirit of people.

Milton Rokeach (1968) and Terrence Deal and Allan Kennedy (1982) speak to values and beliefs as major forces that impact the behavior of groups and individuals. Although values and beliefs underlie our actions, they are often the most ignored and most abused components of our decision making and our actions. Each of us does exceptionally well with our values and beliefs, as long as we stay to ourselves. Each of us is a system, and function effectively as long as we are free of interaction from other systems. However, the intervention of other systems often causes our personal systems to experience some malfunction as the new system does not exactly mesh with ours. This new experience requires that we either assimilate the values and beliefs of the intervening system, influence it to assimilate our values and beliefs, mold ourselves to its way (or it to ours), or become dysfunctional because the systems will not function together. We must be flexible in order to get along with the differences in other people. To some, the basic tenets—the basic beliefs and values—are honesty, truth, and fairness. To others, they are power, control, and loyalty. To still others, they are growth, loving, and equity. Regardless of what the basic tenets are, our actions are focused on upholding and fostering them.

There is a potential problem with the tenets that we hold. They create risks and trials for us in how we relate to the world. We struggle to find others like us, and this struggle is evident in the friends we develop, the church we attend, the significant people that share our lives, and the places we work. Our hope is to make our world and the experiences we have consistent. We like the sameness and fight to keep our lives in equilibrium in order to be comfortable and to find rest from daily tribulations. Unfortunately, changes do take place and are a threat to our comfort. We often see these changes as threats to our beliefs and values. We have taken so much of our world for granted, and change forces us to alter patterns that have appeared functional. In reality, they were just common actions that became habit—and sometimes became dysfunctional—because we used no external points of reference.

Values and beliefs are common threads for successful movement through life. More than one set of values is critical for successfully getting through the day, and ultimately relating to the world. Unfortunately, it appears that society, spiritual groups, family structures, and other groups foster only one set of values and discount others. In response, we attempt to construct our world in order that we experience a smooth transition from one set of values to another.

Consider the following: It is commonly believed that employees are raised by their families to be loving, trusting, and people-oriented. They are raised to believe that people should be trusted and will do the right thing in relation to others and organizational life. These trusting, people-oriented persons begin to work for a utility company that is highly control oriented. The organization's values say that regulatory requirements governing their operation establish a structure which requires that people not be trusted. Public safety requirements and productivity issues guide the organization to view the employees as needing control. The values of the employee and the organization may be in conflict, especially if the employee's emotional and social development is neither sophisticated nor fluid enough to see the validity in different values. Failure to recognize that differences in our values are valid and appropriate sets the stage for conflict, nonresolution, disappointment, disempowerment, and dysfunction if we should be unable to adapt. The outcome is power, abuse, and loss. The outcome is the loss of organizational and personal spirit.

The issue surrounding organizational and personal spirit focuses on the creation of belief systems that frame personal and organizational choices. These choices often involve looking at values; however, their strength is based on the creation of belief systems that establish rational boundaries for thought and action. This process of thought and action is the second component within the trinity—the spirit.

Values structure the way we respond or react to people, situations, or thoughts. Being effective and healthy for both people and organizations involves consistent and congruent matching of values with performance. Incongruent matching of one's values with demonstrable activity creates dysfunction and retards one's potential to match thought, action, motives, feelings, and consequences. If you return to Chapters 1 to 4 of this book, you will remember the issues of psychosis, manic-depression, and codependence. Each establishes a pattern of dysfunction that directly impacts the spirit of organizations and people. Effective spirit development, effective movement in the tripartate system, involves balancing the process paradigms with the spirit base of the trinity process system.

Values cease to be effective and comforting when they are strictly defined. For many, values are based on geographic influence, historical family systems, and peers. Values develop over time, and significant emotional events may solidify or arrest the developmental process—thus, what is perceived as appropriate behavior or thought may not fit the surroundings to which one has become accustomed. Inability to adapt to environmental changes can begin to create dysfunctional behavior and thought.

Value sets are often hard to maintain in a rigid framework when threatened by newness, altering societal norms, or significant emotional events. The church, specifically the Catholic Church, experiences difficulty in promoting its views on abortion, homosexuality, female priests, and other such topics as society alters its views on these same issues. Strict adherence to historical values has enormous negative consequences when cultural and societal values fluctuate to new positions. Demands for adherence to the historical values of the church without valid, current reasoning for maintaining the old view have detrimental effects.

Inconsistency creates enormous dysfunctional activity concerning values. The focal issue is double-standard valuing, which is conditional in nature. Statements such as, "It's okay for Black people to live in my neighborhood but not for them to date my daughter," create confusion and misrepresent the values that seem to be held and followed. Businesses establish double standards in the treatment of employees, the policies that are created (yet applied differently) in the pay process that disempowers equality in the gender compensation, and numerous other examples. If double standards become a way of life for the person and the business, it will be hard to recognize the need to deal with life and its experiences ethically and with integrity.

So what does guide the manner in which we function? What establishes our need to conform to, rebel against, or withdraw from life and the work environment? What creates the traumatic breaks that cause us to experience difficulty in managing ourselves and the change process? Our belief systems are the critical bases more so than our value sets.

THE BELIEF SYSTEMS

Belief Systems

There are numerous beliefs that govern our lives and our actions in our relationships with individuals and organizational systems. There are also beliefs that exist for organizations for how they respond to people, competitors, and short- or long-range plans. Some beliefs are more central and stronger than others. Some beliefs are easily changed, while others support the very fiber of our existence. All the rational information in the world may be wasted if the belief that guides us is violated by rationality.

Beliefs are the primary determining factor for our being functional in our relationships with people or organizational systems. A belief system is the framework that defines each person's or organization's psychological, emotional, and personal structure for explaining physical and social reality. Belief systems determine our motivations, emotions, cognition, affection, perception, thinking, learning, and actions. Beliefs and belief systems can cause changes to be made when an individual or organization experiences positive or negative critical events that impact the way they look at and want to experience the world. Belief systems become our underlying values and our underlying assumptions.

Theological/Legal/Psychological Belief Systems

If one focuses on primitive beliefs as the basis for guiding thoughts, decisions, and actions, then they would fit in one of three categories. I call these categories the belief systems because they define the parameters that guide the way we think, believe, process, and act. These categories are illustrated in Figure 9.4.

The primary belief system or influence broker, which sets the standard for most other beliefs, is the theological belief system, and is based on two components: theoretical beliefs and religious beliefs. The theoretical belief is the insistence that knowledge is the foundation for thought, action, and process. It addresses the concept that control is based on one's command of information. If one is "learned," then one is competent to decide, think, and determine how the world should be. Historically, the "thinkers" were the aristocrats and theologians of society, for they were those who felt they were in the best economic and educational stratum to guide and decide for others. They viewed chaos and disorder as threatening and dangerous to a process of perfection, and therefore determined that leadership must remain in the hands of the knowledgeable.

As knowledge was critical, and the learned of the society were usually members of religious orders, the second belief—the religious—becomes important. The religious belief demands that order and rules become the guiding force of a wholesome society, for only through order and rules can the society perpetuate itself and prosper. Anything that violates the rules threatens the order that has been established. To ensure control, religion must therefore set the standard for appropriate thought, action, and behavior. Witness the strength today of the Catholic Church, the Judaic tradition, the Moral Majority, the Southern Baptists, the television evangelists, and the "Black Church" in governing the actions and decisions of people. The religious belief demands of people that they recognize their finite and dependent nature, and in so doing, demands codependence and subservience to the "higher authority" of the church.

Having defined the church as one influence broker, thought must be given to how the theological belief system is maintained. The legal belief system addresses this issue in that it is comprised of two critical beliefs:

political beliefs and economic beliefs. The purveyors of the religious belief have a need to ensure control over actions and thoughts. The political belief, on the other hand, has as its focus power and authority. If one legislates behavior, thought, and action, and validates it based on the word of a higher authority, then one has placed divine guidance on political action. The political belief places primary importance on the degree of power and authority that one can maintain. Congressmen, bishops, deacons, attorneys, and executive officers are examples of people who predominantly utilize this belief system. The edge is given to people in these positions, as they normally hold theoretical and religious beliefs in secondary importance as baseline guides for political decision making. To ensure that no change occurs in the order of things, the economic belief is brought forth. To discourage change, concern with money, control, and growth becomes the highest priority. If money is in the hands of a few, then control and the order originally established are maintained. Historically, and in present society, the church, legal professionals, theoretical professionals, and economic professionals maintain control over this order.

The psychological belief system is in opposition to the other belief systems, and is composed of the social belief and the emotive belief. The social belief is a focused approach to respecting people as capable and competent in making decisions without being controlled by rules, authority, or power. The primary tenet of this belief is to expunge any conditioning which conveys the notion that one is valued if the tenets of the theological and legal belief systems are followed. It instead focuses on one's ability to belong, care, and "be," simply because one exists in the world. Strategically, the social belief has as its highest order the concern for enhancing one's ability to value and trust based on internal issues rather than external validations. The emotive belief enhances the social belief by placing worth in the ability to merge one's perception of self with one's feelings. It is a process that further reinforces the ability to rely on self and value the potential of others to rely on themselves. It places credence in equality, empowerment, and fairness, and eliminates rule, order, power, and authority as essential components to the "order." Empowerment is a personal process and often runs head-on into the systemic processes of the theological and legal belief systems.

The challenge in these belief systems is to move beyond the narrowness each belief system establishes. Each demands a purity devoid of combinations of the others, and in so doing, creates the possibilities in a subscriber for dysfunctional performance. Each system is either black or white, and avoids looking at any gray areas that exist in merging baselines for effective development and movement within personal and organizational life.

Organizations and people struggle with spirit daily. The concept of living business, living in business, and living with business are all examples of the dynamics that impact development and change. Spirit, as a component of the trinity, has equal value and placement with the process paradigms. How we embrace the developmental process becomes how we understand and hear the spirit that guides or organizational and personal choices. Remember the categories of choice, and remember that the underlying assumptions about living and being in business are driven by the choices we make for the present and future.

SYSTEMS CHANGE: ORGANIZATIONAL DEVELOPMENT/DERIVED BELIEFS

The latest thrust in organizational development is to address an organization as a cultural entity in which it is a total system functioning effectively because it integrates social systems and process systems. The social system is made up of the organizational climate, the communication flow, the role sets of the employees, the decision/authority matrix, and the individuals. The process system is composed of the policies and rules, compensation practices, advancement procedures, and the resource allocation plan. The degree to which these systems are able to work together harmoniously impacts the effective functioning of the organization.

For years, management development and organizational development professionals have stated that organizations function within specified parameters in process systems. If the industry is highly regulated, the policies and rules are clearly defined. The managerial echelon is lofty, and advancement through the ranks is a long, arduous process. If the industry is sales-oriented, the rules and procedures are usually loose to allow maximum flexibility among employees to make decisions and take action. Process has been understood and accepted. However, the professionals have confronted organizations' ability to manage the social systems. Organizations have been challenged in the way they focus on accomplishing the job without regard for the needs and wants of the human being. Challenges concerning emotional wellness of the system have been critical: Has the organization fostered a climate of trust? Are politics playing too large a role in the way business is conducted? Is the atmosphere relaxed, defensive, cautious, or accepting? Is the style of management hurting people? Is there good communication? Are employees motivated enough, or are management's actions causing a lack of motivation?

To address the issues, management theorists have focused on managing by "walking around," participative management, management by objectives, and other techniques. They have challenged decision-making styles and patterns of management (Theory X, Theory Y, Theory Z, participative management, and authoritarian management) and have stressed roles, position, and status. Discussion has centered around communication theory, and emphasis has been placed on the value of the individual. Yet with each new approach, theory, or change, the same situations, conditions, and failings continue to take place. The organization is made responsible for the mistakes of the employees, and the employees are blamed for the failings of the corporation.

Why should one change the organization, system, or methods? Is it to remain current with the new world or is it because one does not understand basic tenets? Why does one fill a position within the organization? What role is played that allows the organization to achieve its goals? Persons within organizations often do not maintain the same belief systems as the organization. Unfortunately, the differences in belief systems create stress and reduce the potential for personal and organizational success. One is usually a leader because one is capable of making things happen while maintaining the beliefs and structures that the organization has established. These persons are typically problem-oriented and make changes through an incremental process, whether or not the incremental process is the most effective choice. Their role and position focus on improving the organization through output and measurable results, while reducing organizational unrest. They struggle to keep the organization and its employees aligned towards the same goals. Change is not essential, but is an additional amenity. The dynamic of spirit is the recognition that assumptions, values, and beliefs govern organizational and personal action. How we choose to embrace that action often dictates what we experience. How we embrace our spirit impacts how we process the development of our organizations and ourselves. How we develop personally and organizationally impacts our understanding of the spirit within us and the spirit within the business. We are joined in the process and ultimately must rely on that connectedness to guide our overall organizational and personal choices and actions.

The beliefs of organizations typically focus on the organization's maintenance. They are derived beliefs, and provide an authority with which one can identify for comfort, stability, and direction. The beliefs of the people within the organization are often perceived by the organization as inconsequential, in that their tastes in matters such as dress code, image, or behavior typically coincide with the beliefs and actions of the corporation, and all other beliefs do not matter. When corporate leadership determines that a systems change is required, they implement it incrementally in order to sustain the beliefs and processes currently in place to reduce the potential challenges to the organization.

Change occurs by data-gathering, analysis, planning, implementation, and evaluation of that data. This process occurs continuously in order to solve a problem, not to create a change. It does not happen arbitrarily. One should not infer from this that employees and leaders of the organization do not change, but rather that the change is small and focused towards resolution of problems that will ultimately impact the organization in positive ways while maintaining the original beliefs and values. Thus, there is no real change, and potentially, there is further damage to the organizational spirit.

CULTURAL CHANGE: ORGANIZATIONAL DEVELOPMENT/PRIMITIVE BELIEFS

A second method exists for assessing and understanding what happens to the spirit in personal and organizational life. Martin Buber, a theologian of much renown, once stated in his book, *I and Thou*, that people have two types of experiences. "I–Thou" experiences are those times and meetings with one's Supreme Being where understanding and thought are one. However, when the individual tries to explain that experience to another person, a portion of the idea is lost in transition, and the idea is not fully explained, understood, or shared. The experience with the Supreme Being becomes an "I–It" experience.

Buber's basic theme is that perspectives, basic assumptions, values, and beliefs guide the nature of people's experiences, and potentially their actions. Thought, analysis of perspectives, assumptions, beliefs, and values are the bases for cultural analysis.

Cultural analysis is the search for the basic beliefs and values that guide the actions and thoughts of organizations. It is the struggle to assess general ideas, commandments, sins, artifacts, myths, and rituals that determine behavior and thought. Perspectives and paradigms are altered, artifacts changed, and myths began to dissipate in the exploration and expansion of "living spirit" in a cultural analysis. Referring to a Black person as "boy," "nigger," or "colored," and "stud" ceased to be acceptable. A revolution had taken place to create a radical shift in beliefs and values. A new cultural view had taken place.

The same process applies to corporations. Consider the case of a utility company making a decision to build a nuclear reactor. Regulatory requirements of utility industries normally establish a rigid, tiered organizational structure to ensure quality and control over decisions. Decision making is therefore slow, and change is very methodical and incremental. However, nuclear energy is an unknown commodity. Decision making in the traditional manner of the utility industry may unduly hamper productivity and, potentially, safety in the nuclear industry. The beliefs and values of the two types of industry—that is, traditional utilities and nuclear energy facilities—will be in conflict. Dysfunctional performance begins to take place because the process systems and the social systems must be different. Shared ideas and actions are different for the employees and management. Assumptions are not the same based on the nature of the industry. Physical artifacts are different. Problems arise. In order to become successful, revolutionary change in the belief systems must take place. Incremental change is therefore inappropriate in its timing. Traditional views and new ideas are in conflict, and a cultural change begins.

Cultural change is value-oriented and unpredictable. It transforms basic assumptions, involves assessing dysfunctional effects of the basic assumptions, is manageable, focuses on the quality of the system, and demands changes in one's leadership and work style to shift to the new view. Each of the examples given in this chapter illustrate these factors for a cultural change.

In each situation, a crisis or significant event has called into question basic assumptions and beliefs. There is a breakdown of the symbols, beliefs, and structure. New assumptions are generated and new leadership emerges. Conflict occurs between the old and new approaches. Unfortunately, cultural change often stops at this point while still incomplete and frustrating. Some additional elements of a comprehensive cultural change are required that are harder to attain. The new leadership must be given credit for the changes. Not giving credit to others, however, is often a failure of the previous leaders in their approach. The new leadership must establish new symbols and beliefs with a new structure. If authority is not given for the changes, however, dysfunction becomes the pattern, and the old symbols, myths, and artifacts remain. Each change, challenge, and exploration is a process of assessing the personal and organizational lifeblood or spirit that governs thought and action.

With the gay, Black, and women's movements, and changes in corporations, changes start out culturally oriented, yet stop short of completion. Incremental, systemic problem resolution becomes the result. All persons within these groups lose, because nothing is completed. Frustration sets in, and each begins to blame the other for the dysfunction that occurs.

Change should be based on the value sets and belief systems held, or on the value sets and belief systems chosen to be altered—not on a new theory, technique, director, leader, or executive. Change is threatening, but is necessary when maintenance of belief systems and value sets gets in the way of performance, effective functioning, and growth.

An important factor in our moving through life gracefully is our ability to match our belief systems with others. We tend to accept and value those persons and organizational entities that have belief systems similar to our own. Political parties, religious institutions, academic institutions, professional classifications, lifestyles, and other major entities in one way or another may hold these similar belief systems. We align ourselves with those authority groups that are most like ourselves. We also align ourselves against those beliefs that seem distant or foreign to our way of functioning, believing, and acting. Marxism, Communism, bigamy, alternative lifestyles, and defense and nuclear industries would be examples of avenues of functioning that go against popular beliefs. The critical factor lies in not judging the differences, but accepting that they are different and moving on to those beliefs that are alike. The critical factor becomes our ability to control how we view what happens in our environment. Attitudes are the meshing of multiple beliefs and values around an action, object, or person that predisposes us to respond to the situations they create. Dislike of nuclear power, hatred of gays, the feeling that women are sex objects, or that management will never look after the "little guy" are all attitudes. None of these may be based in fact; rather, they are based on beliefs and, in that respect, may; be unchangeable.

Each belief we hold guides our functioning and attitudes, and forms the structure for our actions. Each belief is cognitive in its ability to describe the knowledge that we have or perceive about a subject. Each belief is affective because it generates feelings about a subject. Each belief we hold is behavioral because it establishes the types of responses or reactions we will display toward a subject. All organizations and persons struggle to maintain a healthy relationship between their thoughts, feelings, actions, and each belief (or all groups of beliefs) that they hold.

When you struggle to accept a child's interracial marriage, are forced to choose a profession that you would not want to choose, or confront those making decisions that a corporation must alter the way it conducts business, you are struggling to maintain congruence with your beliefs and attitudes because you want to remain comfortable. Vested interest demands that something be done because time and energy on your part was devoted to things becoming or staying the way they are. You have aligned yourself with people, structures, and communities that support your view and you cannot change or do something different without altering your view of yourself and the world; and you have established a spirit within the organization that frames personal and organizational action and decision making.

Cursory responses to these concerns usually include working on motivation, increasing pay, altering managerial styles, or altering the organizational structure. None of these avenues address the beliefs, values, or attitudes of the larger organization. Changes should occur only when one's beliefs, values, and attitudes no longer suffice for the way they perceive the world or the way they choose to operate within the world. Change should occur when one's potential to grow, develop, and prosper is seen as limited or when beliefs, values, and attitudes impair important relationships. However, having beliefs and values challenged often only causes us to regress to our primitive beliefs and communal values to reduce our stress, tension, discord, and potential. This reaction usually creates dysfunction, stress, and an inability to evaluate beliefs and values to assess their continued and potential usefulness.

HUMANITY: BEING PERSONAL IN BUSINESS AND PERSONAL DEVELOPMENT

We have now looked at spirit and its importance to a trinity process for business and personal development. There is one more component of the trinity—the humanity of the trinity.

The humanity within systems is based on the potential of any system to passionately care for itself. Systems are organized approaches to addressing relationships between the parts or elements of the system. Every system has characteristics. The first characteristic is the element or point of description of the system. The element is the nature of work, the product, or a given boundary. In the case of the educational preparation organization, elements were testing outcomes, geographic facilities, policies, and procedures of the organization, human resources, and so forth. All of these elements can be articulated as separate pieces of the whole. The second characteristic is described as the boundary of the system. A boundary is any organizational component that creates breaks between the elements of the system. An example could be different rules for geographic facilities from the rules for the parent company in New York, based on the different elements of the system. The third characteristic of the system is the relationship process within the system. The relations occurring within the system identify associations that exist, such as the interactions of the human resources, the levels of power within the system, or the commonalities of structures within the system. The fourth characteristic is the quality component of the system. The quality component is a description of the system in its entirety which may be different from the parts of the system.

Every organization is a system composed of elements, boundaries, relations, qualities, and causes. Each has created its own pattern of defining its way of being or working in the world. Every organization has effectually created its own paradigm. Psychosis is often the outcome when a dramatic shift begins to occur within the organization that alters the original worldview of that organization. When management changes the structures or the processes or any one or several of the elements of the organization, the expressed changes can create a psychotic shift. Policies that alter the quality of the organization begin a causal process that starts the underlying violence paradigm to begin. This process begins our discussion of humanity—our challenge to embrace the humanness of our actions and its impact on the living development of people within the organization.

Recent thought has defined the shift that occurs from one paradigm to another as *paradigm reconstruction.* Paradigm shifts are not as common as management and consultants would like to believe; rather, paradigm shifts are total system alterations based on impacts to one or more components to the existent system. The process of paradigm reconstruction become the process of humanity within business. Businesses reconstruct themselves to embrace the uniqueness and humanness of its members. Our humanity within business is the exclusion of violence and psychosis, as well as a process of choice.

In my book, *Organizational Violence,* I was particularly drawn to the concept of trauma. I am even more drawn to that concept as our current American society responds to pain, poverty, homelessness, divorce, gangs, violence, and other "social abberations" of our society. In the book, I talked of the creations of violence. The first step for me was understanding the components of the violence paradigm. The components of the violence system are (1) the tenets of violence (such as bonding factors and power factors), (2) the vessels of violence (such as policies, rules, and labor agreements), (3) the structure of violence (such as the lack of systems, rules, appearance, and practice standards), (4) the process of violence (such as circles of control versus circles of influence parameters), and (5) the boundaries of violence (such as balance of power strategies). Each of these components could be set in motion by violation of the components of any existing system. The violence paradigm was, therefore, in existence at all times with any other system or any other paradigm.

Figure 9.7 depicts the relationship of the existing organizational system as the dominant system, with the violence paradigm as a sub-level system just below the existing organizational system. It is important to remember that both systems will exist at all times. The issue becomes ensuring that the violence paradigm does not "rear its head" and become the dominant system in place within the organization; for as the violence occurs, the humanity wanes.

As the violence paradigm operates in tandem with all other paradigms, it becomes important to understand the "trigger" that allows the violence paradigm to become the primary paradigm in existence. The trigger process for the violence paradigm is the lack of a vacuum. Each

Figure 9.7
Coexistent Paradigms

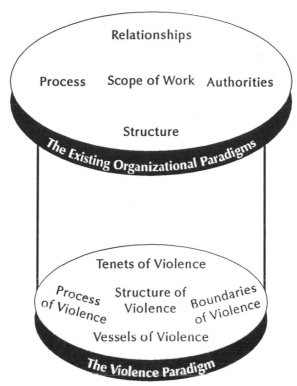

time a shift occurs in the components of systems, space or vacuums are needed for the organization and the person to assimilate the new or different learning. That vacuum becomes the most critical component for suppressing the violence paradigm and energizing humanity. Think of the changes that have occurred in your jobs or work careers. Think how often management had a secret, and thrust that secret upon you at the last minute, demanding a change in your life. Think of the times when your significant other announced a change in the nature of the relationship. Think of the downsizing of any organization—its impact on the elements, boundaries, and quality of the organization. Each time an organization shifts the organizational system without attending to the wholeness of the process of change, the violence paradigm becomes superimposed on the existing system, triggering the violence paradigm.

Simply stated, some key themes frame the humanity of business: inclusion, communication, fairness, involvement, knowledge, meaning, and wisdom. These terms speak to the themes that prevent the violence paradigm from forming in business and among people, thus creating a structure that supports wholeness and congruence as key outcomes in the process of business and people development.

We participate in the dominance of the violence paradigm not because we want to experience violence, but because little attention is given to ensuring that the violence paradigm remains at a sublevel of organizational and personal life. How do we work through a process of violence when it has occurred? How do we traverse the waters of change without initializing the violence paradigm? How do we keep sight of our humanity and well-being so that the violence issues and the psychosis of organizations and people are not upon us?

I believe that our humanity is directly connected with our authenticity. The more we move from being authentic, the more violence and psychosis we experience in our lives. The more congruent we are with our spirit and values—the more we keep sight of the context in which we develop and professionally operate—the more authentic the humanity of our business and our own lives we begin to experience. The aura of calm in our humanity is the point of total authenticity.

Often the process of violence is the underlying factor in choices made within organizations without employees or managers understanding the driving force for their thoughts or actions. Attending to the process of violence is critical for successful change or maintenance of an organization and its members. We, however, need to understand a step-by-step approach to expunging the violence and reframing our authenticity.

THE DISEMPOWERING PROCESS: HOW BEING UNAUTHENTIC BEGINS

The challenge for humanity and the challenge for organizations is the recognition of strategies we employ to disempower ourselves and our potential within organizations. The process of disempowering is a process of disconnecting and disrespecting our heritage, our gifts, and our passions that drive our participation in business or other relationships. Disconnections and disrespect are based on the need to win and often oppress others. Each time we strategize to ensure the defeat of another, set in motion actions that pit people against one another, or find ways to blame and shame another, we set about the process of disempowerment. Disempowerment is the intentional acts established to ensure that one person or one system can defeat another, or the intentional process of disrespecting the freedoms and the values of another. Paulo Freire in *Pedagogy of the Oppressed* states, "Men rarely admit their fear of freedom openly, however tending rather to camouflage it, sometimes unconsciously by presenting themselves as defenders of freedom. But they confuse freedom with the maintenance of the status quo. If anyone places the status quo in question, it thereby seems to constitute a threat to freedom itself." Each challenge to create movement within the individual or the organization system is an act of freedom and an act of the trinity process. Each act to disrespect or alter the action of movement becomes an act of disempowerment. Each act that disempowers destroys the freedom of choice, movement, and thought. The act of disempowering itself thwarts authenticity. The role of the human condition is to transform in order to increase the pursuit of a fuller humanity. Each step that works toward the emancipation of all is an authentic act. Each act that focuses on ensuring that others experience the strengths and gifts of the moment is an authentic act, and each person who works toward enhancing their development and their process without intentionally disrupting or altering someone else's path is being authentic. Freire says, "How can the oppressed [disempowered] as divided unauthentic beings participate in the development of their liberation? Only as they discover that as long as they live in the duality in which to be is to be like, and to be like is to be like the oppressor, this contribution is impossible." As long as the actions of people focus on mirroring the ends crafted by others, as long as the leaders of business focus on strategies that defeat others, the third component of the trinity process is lost.

Becoming Fully Human

If the aforementioned is to occur, humanity must speak loudly about its participation in the decision-making process of business. Participation involves ensuring that the tenets of violence are avoided. The tenets of violence are created because of the absence of key components in the developmental process of people and organizational systems. These key factors are as follows:

1. The ability of people and organizations to effectively create bonds that foster collaboration and inclusiveness.
2. Placing a high value on inclusiveness in sharing among people the process of growth and understanding regarding the desired outcomes of organizations and family.
3. Balancing the need for individuality with the work ethic of team performance.
4. Embracing rather than discounting the introduction of ideas and ideals.
5. Resolving issues of control, power, and authority.
6. Assessing life's dichotomies where choices are made regarding the ends justifying the means versus the means being a critical dynamic toward achieving an appropriate and just end.

Success for humanity focuses on ensuring that the discount of the tenets never appears. People and organizations must become intentional about ensuring that bonding, inclusion, balance, embracing strategies versus discounting strategies, influence versus power, and means versus the ends are the underlying assumptions for all actions.

Too often, employees describe a nonbonding relationship with their employer. Too often, deceit, noncommitment, abandonment, and disrespect on the part of the organization toward the employee is the existing norm of behavior. Bonding represents the glue that forges lasting and effective relationships. Too often, protection strategies are employed by people who feel pushed or shut out. Too often, organizations make decisions that impact employees lives without real inclusion of the employee in the decision-making process. Too often, balance between the individual and the group is lost for the sake of the group. Collaborating and dialoguing with one another is lost to ensure that organization and family power and control is maintained. Too often, discounting—throwing away the views or perspectives of others, or building homogenous organizations—destroys the passion and vision of employees to be effective within the organization. Too often, winning is the outcome; and in winning, someone must lose. Humanity is based on avoiding the traps in discounting the tenets and creating the options.

You might ask, "What happens when the violence tenets are created? What happens to humanity when disrespect, control, discount, exclusion, and ends are the outcomes? What process takes over?"

This process for humanness in organizational and personal life often involves rethinking the strategic objectives or the political realities that significantly influence the direction of the organization. In any case, the power of the instigator for change establishes the framework for the violence paradigm to begin the superimposing process. Take for example a new commissioner within a government. The commissioner was elected on a platform of increasing the diversity of the decision makers within an organization. The commissioner meets with the county administrative officer during the first week of office, dictating that change will occur or the votes will be found to remove him from his position. The commissioner is deeply committed to the inclusion of minorities and/or women to decision-making roles and is unconcerned with any other factors that might impact change. The commissioner is singularly focused on fulfilling a campaign pledge.

The county administrative officer recognizes the crucial force behind the direction from the commissioner and creates a plan of attack. That plan of attack is the beginning of step one in the violence paradigm. The paradigm begins because a request for change has been made and action is focused on the change. Step one looks at the incompleteness of the creation of 100 percent of scope. To define 100 percent of scope, the county administrative officer looks at the desired outcome. In this case, it is the hiring of minority and female decision makers. The county administrative officer assesses what resources are required and what time frame is necessary to achieve the outcome of the commissioner. Upon assessing the scope, he usually factors into the equation the political realities and the strategic perspectives. These are all conscious assessments of the step one process. However, unconscious assessments are also occurring, based on changes being created by the county administrative officer and the county commissioner.

Figure 9.8 indicates that a desired outcome is impacted not only by the conscious assessment of time, resources, and scope, but also by the six-box process of unconscious assessment. In effect, the components of the six boxes are equally important to the successful change process.

Figure 9.8
Step One: Creating the Violence Paradigm

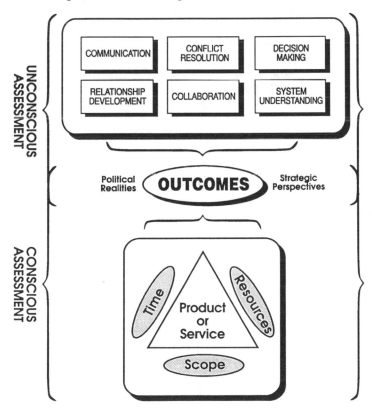

When any one of the unconscious components is overlooked or discounted in the planning process, the violence paradigm begins.

Every employee within the organization begins to trust the organization based on the organization's ability to consistently implement the six components of the unconscious assessment; for in its implementation, the possibilities for humanness are expanded. The unconscious components are the daily actions of employees that guide their experiences of violence or nonviolence—inhumane action or humane action. If the employees experience inconsistency, then the inconsistency begins to trigger issues of lack of trust and confidence, unfairness, and in extreme situations, blame and shame.

Step one began the process of violence. Employees see the change as an issue of management control.

Figure 9.9 shows the control process as experienced by employees. When the change occurs without attending to the unconscious assessment issues, employees experience an expansion of a circle of control. The control circle focuses on I-orientations—for the good of self, not the whole. The more control is expanded, the more employees within the organization experience mistrust, miscommunication, inconsistency, noncongruence, politics, incompetence, and combative behavior. In effect, the expansion of control becomes a process of disempowerment. Change is successful because of careful attention to the tenets of violence.

Step two of the violence system occurs when anyone impacted by the change requests clarification regarding the outcomes desired within the change process. Each time clarification is requested, yet the answer given comes from the circle of control, the violence paradigm is escalated. In step one, the tenets and vessels of violence are experienced by employees; in step two, the structure and process of violence become the strategies that escalate the system. The structure of violence is comprised of the varying standards that impact organizational functioning. In the case of the violence paradigm, standards are nonexistent.

The process of violence occurs through movement from the circle of influence toward the circle of control. The movement occurs because an aura of chaos has taken control of the organizational environment. The circle of control is actualized by the concept of inconsistency and noncongruence. Any action that appears I-oriented becomes a self-serving act. That act suggests that looking out for another is of very low value and protectionist behavior must be actualized. All actions are suspect, all behavior is mistrustful, and all statements seem to have hidden meaning. Teamwork, collaboration, and we-oriented action have dissipated. Let us try and walk through the process of violence in Figure 9.10.

The circle of control operates from the perspective that self-serving behavior demands a winner and a loser. The I-oriented person is unclear

Figure 9.9
Control Parameters

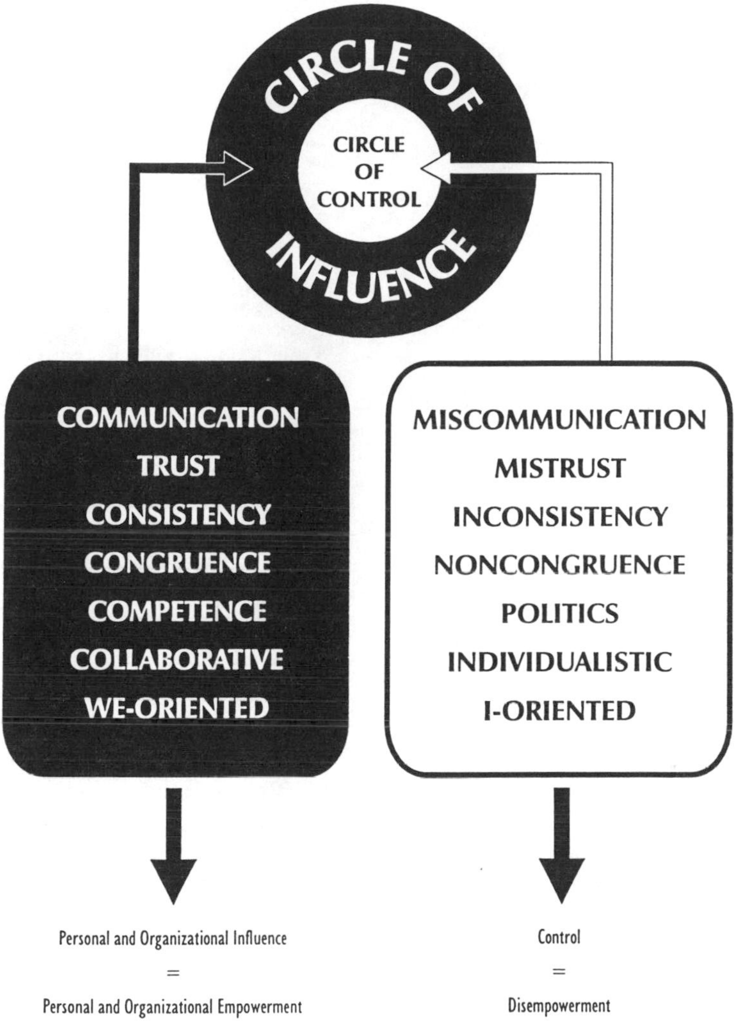

CIRCLE OF INFLUENCE

CIRCLE
OF
CONTROL

COMMUNICATION	MISCOMMUNICATION
TRUST	MISTRUST
CONSISTENCY	INCONSISTENCY
CONGRUENCE	NONCONGRUENCE
COMPETENCE	POLITICS
COLLABORATIVE	INDIVIDUALISTIC
WE-ORIENTED	I-ORIENTED

Personal and Organizational Influence

=

Personal and Organizational Empowerment

Control

=

Disempowerment

in their communication and behaves inconsistently, altering behavior to ensure that only one perspective is valued or heard.

Think of all the times you have tried to do the right thing, only to experience an explosion because the process was so wrong; and the times you believed your strategy for making a change was just perfect, only to experience a misfortune. Think of the times people have gotten angry

Figure 9.10
Process of Violence

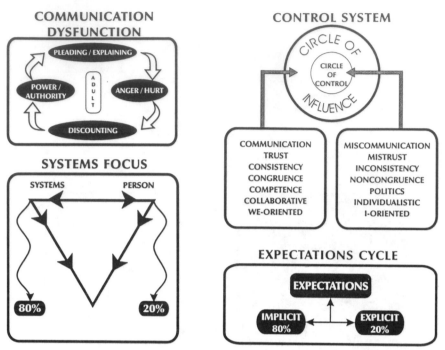

with a plan that you had, even though the plan seemed to make perfect sense. In each situation, the degrees of anger had nothing to do with your plan or strategy—the anger came as a result of your process. Such is the case with the violence paradigm. In each of the steps to this point, the rationale, the strategy, was not at issue; the process was the catalyst for the violence. Therefore, the violence paradigm is a process paradigm. The process coexists with everything else you can create, and based on the processes you create to achieve an outcome, the violence paradigm emerges as supreme in reaction to the processes you have placed in motion. Bush was not necessarily wrong in the strategies he created to assist America in achieving economic health; it was his insensitivity—his process—that infuriated people. Clinton may not have more effective plans than the Republicans; it is his process—his style—that people trust. His path appears to have more equity, his approach creates more bonds, his strategy appears more inclusive, his language suggests a willingness to listen rather than discount, and his programs indicate a justifiable end with well-thought-out means. In effect, Clinton's approach to systems and societal change seems less violent.

The step-by-step approach to the creation of violence is based on a selfish, "my-way-only" process. When actions taken by business or government impact others, yet the others are not included in the development of the strategy, violence becomes the only real outcome. The violence occurs because we forget to pause, to create the necessary vacuum that allows each person or organizational entity to process the impending change. We move in haste to create a change without creating a process that values bonding, inclusion, and acceptance of others' ideas and ideals. We move in haste without ensuring a level of equity and equality, devoid of power, control, and authority. We move in haste, taking little time to assess the impacts of our decisions, thereby often creating unjust means and unjust ends. Each time we create these kinds of steps, we embrace the violence paradigm—the process paradigm as the desired outcome for our actions. We embrace dysfunctional communication as the communication of choice. We embrace the circle of control as the operational strategy of choice, and we embrace the lack of standards as the methodology for addressing any and all concerns from employees, stakeholders, or the general public, ensuring that inconsistency and noncongruence are the appearance standards one can trust.

Whether one evaluates classic, dynamic, communication, field, or evolutionary paradigms, discounting the violence paradigm would make successful outcomes of the theory impossible.

The Prescriptive Process of Nonviolence: Building Humanness

If the discounting process, circle of control, and lack of standards are key elements of the violence paradigm, then the converse of each of those elements become the key components to the nonviolence paradigm. Figure 9.5 depicts the nonviolence paradigm and its role in building humanity.

The violence paradigm occurs because management pays little attention to ensuring that the tenets of violence are effectively managed in the process of change and maintenance within organizations. Each time a change process is considered, management needs to assess the health of the organization. In assessing the health of the organization, management must examine the bonds between the employees and the organization. Has the organization been caring toward employees by instituting meaningful and rewarding training programs? Has the organization looked at career paths and promotion strategies? Has the organization instituted employee recognition and involvement programs? Has the leadership of the organization provided opportunities for employees to be heard?

Management must also assess the degree to which the organization has involved employees in the planning and decision-making process. The issue for management in the assessment is one of inclusion. Has management looked at a process of inclusion by all employees in the development and implementation of the work scope? Has management performed employee attitude surveys to discover the real issues for employees? Has management taken to heart the concerns raised by employees and acted on the issues, rather than give the appearance of lip service? Has management determined strategies to ensure that the worth and gifts of the individual are balanced by the recognition of the team? Has management embraced the strength of the individual in a noncompetitive manner? Has management looked at the creation of multitalented employees to ensure the diversity of assignments for employees? Has management drawn on the diversity and cultural perspectives of their employees to provide alternatives to approaching problems? Has management prepared the organization to embrace diversity? Are ideas from employees given serious consideration? Are employees' ideals and perspectives really acknowledged? In effect, has management made the employees real and viable partners in the creation, maintenance, and expansion of the organizational system?

Often what occurs within organizations are "yes" answers to some of these questions. The violence paradigm occurs because organizations have not answered *all* of the questions. The violence paradigm is not a piecemeal paradigm, it is an all-or-none paradigm. Addressing each facet is essential to expunging the paradigm.

Achieving authenticity and humanity requires the creation of the aura of calm within the person and the organization. This is not an easy task, yet it is critical for the emotional health of the person and the business system. To create the aura of calm, movement to change should be halted so that time is available to repair the existing organizational paradigm. The aura of calm is the critical intervention for health. It is almost tantamount to physicians stating that sleep is the best medicine for injury. The body needs time to heal itself. The aura of calm is the sleep process within organizations. Use the sleep time to review the tenets of violence. Create a new strategy for bonding, including, listening, embracing difference, and expunging power, control, and authority issues. Then look at how the organization rationalizes and justifies its actions, recognizing that creating a just end is essential to organizational health. Once the aura of calm is in place and strategies for reparations are underway, then look at the structures of violence.

The structure of violence focuses on the lack of standards. To expunge the structures of violence, assess the existence of standards within the organization. To expunge the violence, a concerted effort is required to create standards. The creation of standards does not destroy creativity;

rather, it creates the environment and establishes the organization ethos that guides and governs both what we will accomplish and the way we will accomplish work. Every organization—public, private, or non-profit—has system standards. Politics is an inevitable fact of organizational life. The creation of system standards helps in the development of a strategic direction for the organization. From that strategic direction, an organization is poised to realistically craft rules standards. Standards are based on guiding principles that impact the direction of all policies, procedures, and administrative regulations. This would mean that negotiated labor agreements, personnel policies, departmental operating procedures, civil service agreements, payroll policies, and supervisory and management rules are all guided by the systems standards; and as rules standards, they must match. Too often, organizations create policies at the top end and violate the policies at every other turn within the organization. Once assessments have occurred in each of these areas, charting of the discoveries have been noted, and three components of the violence system have been identified. Management is now ready to embrace a system of nonviolence.

We have come full circle. Balancing the human paradigm with the organizational history creates the existing organizational system. The process of violence elimination assesses the organizational history, the human history, and the outcome of change to create a new organizational paradigm that values and embraces humanity as a key partner in the process of business and personal development.

THE COMPETENCIES: REQUIRED SKILLS FOR SUCCESS

We have talked about the trinity process: its humanity, spirit, and context. What has not been addressed are the competencies that people in business need to be effective and succeed. Figure 9.6 focused on the competencies that business members need to embrace the trinity. As the trinity embraces human/psychological development, theoretical/philosophical development, and spiritual/value-based development, the competencies are framed in the same manner.

Three areas of expertise are essential for living businesses to transform. Theologically, the concept of the trinity is one of transformation, and the experience of Buber's I–Thou is based in part on the creation of skills that allow success in business.

Theoretical/Philosophical Competency

Primary in the development of competency is the recognition that all of the skills within the framework are needed for success. In this competency are the technological skills that ensure the survivability of business. Financial management, marketing and sales, research and development (including scientific, heuristic, and appreciative inquiries), information management, human resource management, strategic planning, resource management, inventory management and distribution, public works, construction and engineering, or any other specific or specialized skill is essential to this process. Unfortunately, businesses tend to focus on the specialty, allowing it to become the primary direction of the business process.

Success in business is based on the integration of data, procedures, functions, and management. Therefore, reliance on one specialty over another causes businesses to hear data from one group over another. A lopsided outcome becomes inevitable. Consider a utility corporation that sees the production of water as its highest need. Departments of water planning, engineering, water operations, and construction are essential specialties for the organization. Decision making is framed by these four departments; yet the organization finds itself strapped by the actions of these departments, because it did not equally value finance, human resources, public information, customer service, and other departments. The thoughts and views of the water planning, water operations, engineering, and construction departments were more important. Over time, fiscal management, resource management, public perception, and customer quality were the areas where complaints and problems arose. The problems occurred because equal value and resources were not provided to the departments that needed to support the business outcomes. Fragmentation and compartmentalization were the driving decision makers, and the organization as a whole was the loser.

Every employee needs to understand minimal strategies in each of the technological skills, so that decisions consider the impacts of each area before finalization. This is critical to transformation. Our personal and professional competency zones need to expand in order for effective business development to occur.

Human/Psychological Competency

Technical competency is not enough for businesses to be successful. The often-forgotten dynamic is the human and psychological component of business decision making and performance. Therefore, each leader in business must acquire some skill and proficiency in the human/ psychological dimension. Organizational development, communication (interpersonal, intrapersonal, organizational, oral, and written), conflict management, networking, process consulting, group behavior, organizational behavior, team development, career development for individuals, and collaborative modeling allow for a holistic approach to the management of people and systems. Technical skills speak to the compartments of business, as human skills speak to the management of the work and the development of the people accountable for the work.

Too often, managers and executives discard these human psychological skills as the "fluff" of the organization. Nothing is further from the truth. In Long Beach, California, the city manager determined that a rotation of executives from department to department every two years would be an excellent process of acquainting all the directors with all the areas of city government. Initially, he met with significant resistance because the directors were espousing technical proficiency over human psychological proficiency. The city manager utilized the skills of the human/psychological dimension to influence the directors to try the process. Over time, the directors recognized that their success was based on their proficiency in the human/psychological dimension more than the theoretical/philosophical dimension. Each was important, but the human/psychological skills were transferable from department to department.

Spirit and Value-Based Competency

The context in which learning and transformation occur for business is the overriding dynamic in successful business. Blending personal and organizational values, expanding organizational horizons to embrace global change and global living, preparing for change in the members of organizations where persons of diverse backgrounds and cultures will frame the workforce, moving from closed processes to learning organizations, recognizing the belief systems that guide personal and organizational performance, and defining the spirit of the organization are all essential for the creation of personal and organizational stability.

When organizations and their members are clear about the values that should frame decisions, when organizations understand the belief structure that guides action, when employees experience policies and procedures that are inclusive and trust based, or when culture diversity and global recognition frame business and strategic planning, organizations and people feel energized and excited about the business process.

All three competencies are necessary for successful business, and all three must be held by all members of the organization. Training, seminars, policy and procedure planning, self-directed work teams, transformation teams, and learning organization meetings all prepare the employee and the organization to work in concert with each other, rather than create violent paradigms. All prepare the employee and the organization to remain focused on the underlying assumptions, values, and purposes of the organization, and prepare the systems and people to recognize when actions are outside the scope of the process paradigms.

We are at the nexus of transformation and change. We are at the core of business success and people effectiveness. We are at an understanding of the trinity process, and how it can immeasurably change and alter our understanding of the work world and its impact on people and systems.

UTILIZATIONS OF THE TRINITY PROCESS

CHAPTER 10

Changing the Human and Business System Outcomes

The trinity process is a system of transformation and learning. Its underlying assumption is that people and systems develop over time without end, thereby creating opportunities for change and growth on a continuum of life. The process of development is a tripartate system of spirit, context, and humanity, and its competencies are in three primary domains. Some primary thoughts become important here in the frame of learning and change.

My lifelong professional outcomes have been as an organizational development consultant, professor of business and organizational transformation, and as an author. One of the professional disciplines along my own continuum has been as an Episcopal priest. There is a level of comfort for me in coming full circle in the development of business process paradigms, belief systems paradigms, and humanity paradigms that can govern personal and organizational thought and action. As stated earlier, the concept of the trinity is a concept of transformation. Theologically, the concept of trinity—tripartatism—is a path of development and change. Legally, the concept of moralism and structure has guided business and personal action for centuries. Psychologically, the struggle to remain whole has often been wrought with peril, because no real systemic process has been developed that mirrors the issues of the trinity. Focus on profit, control, maintenance, power, authority, or a chaos-free society have usually crafted homogeneity, winners and losers, and aristocrats and paupers, for there has been a devaluing of the mysteries and the infinite process of the development and continual nature of the universe. Not meaning to sound omnipotent or God-like, there is some measure of comfort in recognizing that business, like the universe, continues and transforms.

Remembering your history and geology classes, recollect that transformation of the landscape happens continually. The waters of the universe transformed the landscape and created the Grand Canyon. The changes of the ages caused the existence of the dinosaurs to cease in our world. The building of businesses caused changes in the business landscape every time there is a new merger. The changing of the guard in organizational leadership usually marks a new era for business. In effect, there is always change and transformation, so it is somewhat difficult to understand the fear and trepidation that society and business experience whenever change is imminent.

Each transformational process throughout history has been based on the holistic movement to a different, and often better, framework than the previous one. The excitement in the change historically is that the difference will somehow be better. To that end, the fight against transformation is a fight to restrict and control the natural transformation of the world. The fight against transformation is a fight to ensure the past, not the present and the future. The fight against transforming business is a fight for power over another, thereby creating fragmented, detached, compartmentalized, and dysfunctional systems because the evolutionary process of development and change is stunted for personal gain and personal control.

TRANSFORMATION AS SAVIOR

The sadness in the control process is that one must be perfect; for without perfection, blame and shame are the only methods of explaining divergent experiences. Without transformation, everyone becomes stunted and stagnant. Without the potential to transform, evolve, and develop, we feed on ourselves, destroying any opportunity for renewal. We become addictive and psychotic beings, and thus create addictive and psychotic organizations and businesses. As we recognize the existence of a higher power, we can recognize that business needs to embrace a higher concept. Transformation is that higher concept. Evolution, development, and transformation are the higher powers of business.

It would therefore appear that transformation becomes our saving grace as a species and as intuitive and intelligent beings. We need transformation if we are to live. Business needs to continually embrace transformation if it is to live and thrive.

UTILIZATIONS OF THE TRINITY PROCESS

Planning and Strategy Development

When I think of how I have used the trinity process, I am initially drawn to its usefulness for planning activities within organizations. I am not thinking of strategic planning here. I am thinking of the impact of the process paradigms on the choices that we make in the planning of new products, services, locations, and ventures. The trinity process establishes a comprehensive strategy for identifying, reframing, evaluating, and implementing planning strategies. It is a new technology, and I have found it extremely helpful in communication, decision making, collaborative approaches, relationship building, conflict resolution, strategic planning, diversity inclusion, and profit-defining strategies. It has been helpful in the development of comprehensive system approaches that focus on construction, transition, and implementation. It has helped me with clients in defining the limits of comfort and the expansions of boundaries that heretofore were avoided for fear of control loss. Policy development, executive development, management development, strategic thinking, critical thinking, systems development, and data analysis have all been impacted by the utilizations of the trinity process.

Policy Development

Policies are usually developed to form boundaries for thought and action. This boundary development usually restricts actions and operations within organizations. In so doing, often the creativity within the organization is short-circuited because of the need to control the extent to which change and interpretation within organizations can occur. Think of what would occur for your organizations if policies were developed to foster and support the potential of the organization and its members to invent, create, and change as the information connections generated new ideas and ideals for the organization and its people.

The trinity process allows organizations and leaders to frame the nature of policy development around key principles of growth and development rather than compliance and control. The trinity process can frame how decision making occurs with attention given to the underlying spirit, humanity, and context of change and development. The humanity component of the trinity process would focus on whether the policies build on congruence and inclusion. The context component of the trinity process would assess the congruence between the interpretations, reciprocities, commitments, equalities, empowerments, and representations of the business choices and decisions. The spirit component would look at the underlying belief structures of the organization. Based on the assessments in all three dimensions, decision makers could create policies that ensure organizational rule congruence with the underlying paradigms that guide the history and the current actions of the organization.

Executive Development

If executives are chosen because of their ability to get things accomplished, then those who operate from a framework that drives organizational and personal development have the potential to create organizational and personal action that enhances the long term outcomes of the organization with inclusion of the members accountable for the actions. This is a critical utilization of the trinity process.

The process discussed in this book becomes a trust-based approach to organizational and personal change without ends. Constant renewal, synergy, and dialogue become the frameworks for executive action and accomplishment of outcomes. This technology benefits organizations in assessing the combined strengths of all the executives and determining where differences are too great to be effective. It creates an effective approach to organizational and personal change that allows the executives to empower the organization. The executive must be accountable for the changes and the strategies that make differences matter and succeed.

Recently I watched a group of executives flounder because new leadership had taken over the organization. The executives were historically disempowered to make choices and decisions. They had been selected to head organizational units because they worked best by following orders. Unfortunately, the new executive manager expected them to be empowered managers, poised to make decisions that effectively developed the employees and the service-based issues of the company. They were without the knowledge to achieve the outcomes of the executive manager. I was asked to help them reframe their ways of knowing and acting. The trinity process allowed them to effectively frame thought into action. This process allows managers and employees to embrace their fears and histories to create new ways of being and behaving. Focusing on the spirit, humanity, and context of organizational and personal knowing significantly frames the possibilities and opportunities for the future.

Assessment of baseline beliefs, basic assumptions about humanity, and basic paradigms for operating can help organizations in choosing or developing the right employees, policies, and projects that further the systems of the organization, rather than fight the systems of the organization. Not assessing congruence between organizational outcomes and organizational actions can lead to problems down the road which may become impossible to alter and correct.

Strategic Planning

It is difficult to conceive of a strategic planning process that does not assess the levels of congruity that drive organizational futures. The trinity process allows organizations to realistically understand the present to craft a new future. Issues of mission assessment, values auditing, strategic business modeling, gap analysis, functional outcome assessment, and congruence matching are all enhanced by the trinity process. The trinity process technology assists organizational planners, decision makers, stakeholders, and organizational implementers in their planning processes. Underlying paradigms and assumptions become framed in a contextual manner that allows success.

Strategic planning is the lifeblood of organizational planning. Focusing on that planning without a perspective of values, beliefs, process, and value for the humanity of the organization will often lead to an unsuccessful organization and a violence paradigm. Therefore, alteration of that process can create significance for each and every member of the organization.

Recently, I met with a large transit organization that was looking at its strategic planning process. The organization was recognizing some shortfalls in revenue and had begun to make decisions that focused on monetary survival. The organization began a massive layoff program to address the monetary shortfall, creating a fear-based organizational process where protection was the primary outcome for each employee and manager. The organization simultaneously shared with the strategic-planning team that they could look realistically at any strategy within the organization to frame their thinking and action. The mental picture for the employees on the team was that organizational decision making had already been accomplished and the humanity of the organization was lost in the decisions that had been made.

When the consultation with the trinity process was completed eight months later, the employees and managers felt more focused toward a congruent organizational and personal choice process. A blended approach that focused on personal humanity, organizational context, and personal and organizational spirit drove the decision making and organizational action, rather than a short-focused, incremental decision process that was the history of the organization.

Communication Modeling

Communication and dialogue are the mainstay of any organizational process. What an organization hears and perceives about issues, history, people, and actions drives how it embraces and understands new actions, thoughts, and processes. If the history of the organization does not value shared processes of interaction, then communication may be perceived as a one-way process of control and power that devalues and disempowers employees to think or act. Communication is influenced by environment, family history, culture, ethnicity, and one's underlying paradigms for thought and action. It therefore becomes important that people and systems consider the communication processes in operation.

The trinity process allows the organization and the person to frame communication with a clear framework of the driving and restraining forces in the communication and dialogue cycle. If communication is a personal process of waiting to be heard, and you interface with a person whose communication history is shouting to participate, you may find that the styles impede effective communication. If, however, you can identify the values and strengths of communication that frame the importance of the communication process within an organization, you can alter the strategies historically employed. The trinity process allows that change to occur in the development of a system element. Communication becomes a key system element that is embodied in the development of the organizational system.

Whole Earth Models and Systems

In the 1980s, computer modeling became a critical way of knowing in the global economy. That strategy for knowing focused on the concept of systems as massive computers containing vast arrays of information for every issue that man could produce. The computer models focused on closed-end–based paradigms for developing strategies for problem solving and environmental management. The first model by MIT looked at systems dynamics framed by the physical limitations of the planet. The second model, called the World Integrated Model from Case Western Reserve, focused on multilevel hierarchical systems theory which was input–output driven. The problem resolution was based on resource depletion. The third model was a Latin American World Model. It looked at strategies for optimization with maximum human need as the driving parameter. The MOIRA, a model of international relations in agriculture, was developed with econometrics as the framework for action. The outcome was to develop policies to eliminate hunger in the world. The United Nations Model was developed to address input–output strategies that looked at equity and the environment. All of the strategies were effective to a point; however, none of the computer models were effective because the parameters within the model were limiting.

The trinity process allows strategic thinkers and think-tank analysts to more effectively frame the issues included in modeling. Human, spiritual, and contextual dynamics that are not end-based allow the modeling process to evolve as the issues of the global society evolve. This becomes important for the long-term future of the society.

Systems Thinking Issues

Peter Senge, the author of *The Fifth Discipline*, has developed numerous thinking strategies that are now used in corporations worldwide. Senge's models are designed to help managers think through superficial symptoms to assess the underlying causes of organizational problems, reorganize perceptions into a more congruent picture of the organizational dynamics, and develop ways of knowing that ultimately speed up the process of learning for others. He developed mapping mental models to ensure that organizations would understand the current dynamics guiding organizations. Challenging and reality checking are key components of the mental modeling process.

The trinity process helps mental modeling in its ability to go beneath the dynamics of organizational thinking to the underlying assumptions and paradigms driving organizational dynamics. It is not enough to look at the dynamics of organizations without understanding the paradigms that drive business values and beliefs, organizational strategies about the basic values of people, and key assumptions about the paradigms driving organizational processing. The trinity process addresses these issues.

Guiding ideas, challenging politics, being intellectual, thinking strategically, and being philosophical are current anathemas to organizational process, yet they are the only strategies that can ultimately save organizations. Organizations survive and grow because they are wise, not smart. The trinity process emphasizes being wise, not smart.

THE TRINITY PROCESS IN ACTION

CHAPTER 11

XYZ Corporation's Desire for Congruence and Wholeness—The Balance Option

The development of new paradigms for personal and organizational action often leaves people in a quandry about how to implement the changed approach. The process of utilizing the trinity process is exactly that—a process. This is not a set system that says you have to follow a step-by-step approach, but is a system that suggests that having the answers is not required; rather, that one look at the process of development and change and utilize the process to live with development instead of controlling it.

In my process of seminary training and ordination, I remember the wonderful experience of learning that I did not have to have the answers, just a strategy for framing the questions and walking through the process of discovery. The trinity process is similar in its attention to the fluid continuums of development. Whether one focuses on the humanity dimension and the creation of calm by attending to the elimination of the tenets of violence, the spiritual dimension where underlying beliefs and values guide the thinking and action, or the contextual dimension where people and system change through congruent choices, the importance of process is critical. Cause and effect do not drive this system. Rules and order do not drive this system. Change without consideration of the human dimension does not drive this system. Evolution without attention to change does not drive this system. Growing and development, attending to the movement cycles, understanding, and embracing humanity, living spirit, and clarity of context drive this system.

What follows is a case study of an organization that is currently utilizing the trinity process to frame organizational performance and change. Key to the selection of this process was the underlying assumption that employees are important. The underlying spiritual desires of the executive of the organization are driving the need for organizational action. These criteria for help push charge selection caused XYZ Corporation to focus on the issues of change that were not being addressed by the consultations that focused on the "pieces of the organization" or on "problem solving." The executives wanted a consultation that allowed them to "truly partner with the consultant to explore and discover the mission and value of the organization and the path that service needed to take for the present and future." They liked the concept of process paradigms with process consultation. They appreciated the blend of humanity, spirit, and context. They desired a process where the process created new paradigms and new underlying assumptions. They selected the trinity process.

CASE STUDY OVERVIEW

Following is a case study of one of my current clients. XYZ is a mental health state organization in a southeastern state. The organization is comprised of the departments of retardation and mental health with state offices in four cities. The offices are accountable for administration, client services, protective services, community mental health center liaison services, staff development and training, community outreach services, and higher education liaison services. Each office has traditionally operated as a separate state agency with a office staffing plan of an assistant director for mental health and mental retardation, a manager of mental health, a manager of mental retardation, supervisors of administration, client services, protective services, community mental health center liaison, staff development and training, community outreach services, and higher education liaison services. Each office has been very strong in the area of community outreach services, and the focus in this area has strongly helped in the development of significant political ties to the state legislature in the procurement of funds for their particular catchment areas. Additionally, these political ties have contributed to the inability of the last three directors of mental health being unable to change the organizational structure of mental health and mental retardation, change the staffing of the four offices, and change the culture of the state department.

Twelve months ago, the state legislature appointed a new director of mental health and mental retardation. The person was given a charge by the governor to "change the culture of this organization within three years. It has become a monolith that is too costly, too entrenched and too out of touch with the upcoming changes in mental health and mental retardation. I won't tell you what to do, but I want a permanent change!"

The director of mental health spoke with the last three agency directors to discover the pitfalls in their attempts to change the agency. They sighted inhumane treatment of staff, poor planning in the four catchment areas for budget and program development, too much emphasis on mental retardation and hospital services, and too-powerful managers in the four catchment areas. In fact, they stated that politics made it impossible to alter the situations of the organization. The director recognized that he had a tiger, and he was not sure that he wanted to grab it by the tail. He believed that he had to craft a totally different strategy if he wanted to in any way impact the current culture of the organization. In addition, he felt that the current structure might not be the problem, rather, the people and the stakeholders could be creating the issues. He wanted a consultant and, through an exhaustive search, hired Lloyd C. Williams & Associates because of the use of the trinity process for consultation strategies.

Primary Case Scenarios in Action

As the consultant, I met with the director of mental health and mental retardation to dialogue about the issues perceived and the desired outcomes of the organization. The director stated, "The culture of this organization is hierarchical and controlling. This is a mental health agency and it needs to change, or we'll create in our staffs the same issues that impact our clients. This has to change. I am uncomfortable with the degree of power that my four assistants have in their respective catchment areas, and I need to defuse that power in order to create a change within the organization."

The issues for the director were driving him to seek massive systems change in a transformative manner that would allow some level of congruity on the parts of the staff. To achieve this direction, we sought to have a five-part intervention beginning that would allow the managers and staff to recognize that their roles and their influence were altering.

First, and most important, was identifying for staff the critical concerns of the director. Second was communicating the process for the dialogues that were to occur to the staff. Third was identifying the areas of concern that were impacting effectiveness for the organization. Fourth was reframing the nature of the organization—one entity rather than four. Fifth was determining skill sets or required skills for effectiveness within the organization. The compilation of issues suggested a different mental model for organizational action within the mental health agency.

Strategic Thinking Issues for the Consultation

The issues raised suggest that a paradigm shift within the organization was necessary in order to reframe (1) the outcomes of the agency, (2) the roles of the members of the agency, (3) the structure of the agency, (4) the process for performing work, and (5) the relationships of the four catchment areas within the agency. These five perspectives were critical in driving the development of a different mental model for the agency.

Outcomes of the Agency

The director's perspective on change revolved around the ability of the agency to look long term at differing therapeutic and community modalities for responding to client and community needs. Mental health as an industry was changing. Issues of brief psychotherapy, partnering systems at the client and community level, transitional living, and differing measurement processes were moving mental health as an industry and a profession from the traditional in-patient hospital model and from the traditional community mental health center model to a model of individual assessment and development devoid of a community psychology model. These models focused on the ability of the state agency to define and frame change and development in clients, and to frame how community mental health centers had to be structured to respond to the structure of the state agency. Rather than a proactive and developmental model, the organizations throughout the state had been forced to create a control-based structure to respond to a control-based system of sickness and health.

To move to the different model, the mental map had to focus on health and wellness: fluidness versus control, change versus static structure, eclectic skills versus disciplined specific skills, and alteration of the underlying assumptions about clients and the organization. In effect, there had to be a change of the underlying values and beliefs of the organization.

Roles of the Members of the Agency

The existing roles of the members of the organization focused on father–child relationships. The former directors and the current managers of the catchment areas were the fathers of the organization. All staff beneath them were the children, and they learned skills in being conditionally based fathers to the clients and the community agencies. The structure was up and down with some levels of the paradigm operating from "children are to be seen and not heard." The intent of the role structure was to create a groupthink/one voice approach to mental health and mental health service delivery. Irrespective of the existing skills of the staff in social work, psychology, psychiatry, psychiatric nursing, and medical care, one voice was required for retention of one's position within the state agency.

There is a loss of creativity in the approach that existed for the employees in the agency. Issues of codependence, frustration, depression, anger, and psychosis were emerging among the staff because of the punitive nature of free will and free thinking within the organization. The employees were beginning levels of rebellion through exploration of employee unions, work slowdowns, high absenteeism, and lots of redo work.

Structure of the Agency

Control was a key underlying assumption of organizational structure at the state level and within the four catchment areas of the organization. Top-down structural parameters had been created within the organization. The leaders of the organization stated that the structure was needed to effectively comply with federal and state regulations governing the effective management of mental health. They also believed that it allowed for consistency in interpretation of the rules and the policies of the organization.

They acknowledge that there are difficulties with the communication of information and strategies with the four catchment areas. The catchment areas operate currently as their own "state agencies," wielding power and influence over the mental health relationships within the communities they serve and provide resources to them.

Different structures have been proposed over time; however, no change has occurred because of the power of the catchment area managers. Therefore, the structure has existed in its current format for the past twenty-seven years.

Process for Performing Work

Current processes for performing work involve the following of clear, standard operating procedures. Deviation from the structured format for diagnosis, treatment planning, treatment delivery, or evaluation of clients is not allowed. Diagnosis is done by psychiatrists and psychologists. Testing, measurement, and dispensing of medication are their only functions. Social workers and psychiatric nurses provide therapy. Physicians take care of medical needs, and everyone else down to the janitors supports the work of the professionals.

A hierarchical structure for performing work is the norm within the organization. When a change needs to occur for a client, the proposed strategy must go through the chain to the psychiatrist in charge. If he is not available, the psychologist prepares a temporary decision for use with the client until the psychiatrist determines the appropriate strategy. Decision making is in the hands of the professional only. This includes the turning of patients for treatment of bed sores.

Relationships of the Four Catchment Areas

The north, south, east, and west catchment areas currently operate as their own fiefdoms. Rules from the state are perceived as guidelines, not rules, by the four managers. They have each worked for the mental health state agency twenty-plus years. They have forged relationships with politicians and influential business leaders in their communities, and they view themselves as lords and masters of their domains. From a relationship perspective, relationships among them are tentative; yet there is a comraderie based on the desire to maintain power and control over their domains.

There is an additional comraderie present as a negative perspective about the new director. The managers have forged a pact that is designed to thwart the new director's efforts to instigate change. This perspective on their part is also based on their belief that the state will not make changes quickly. Unless the director can accuse them of inappropriate moral character issues, they sense that they will be able to thwart the process of change through political intervention.

There is some truth to the perspectives of the managers. History supports their perspective. Each time a director has tried, he or she has failed, and the governor of the state has relieved the director of the responsibilities. In their eyes, therefore, the situation is status quo. No matter what the director tries, they can stop the process; so business as usual is the operative phrase.

THE TRINITY PROCESS: INTERVENTION AND CHANGE STRATEGY

The value of the trinity process is its nonjudgmental nature in helping people and systems explore options for change and development. In this intervention, the tripartate system of development and change looks at the issues simultaneously. First in the process is the assessment of the underlying assumptions and values that drive the actions of the organization and its leaders.

The trinity process focuses on the impacts of congruence in the belief systems, calm in the nonviolence paradigm, and wholeness and congruence in the process paradigms for personal and organizational performance. In the case of XYZ Corporation, these three areas of intervention are critical to the overall successful outcomes desired by the organization. Let us start with the underlying assumptions and beliefs of the organization.

The Spirit: Living Systems

The current belief system in operation is a theological and legal belief structure. The theological belief system focuses on the requirement of an organization or people to have as the highest need and highest value the compliance with rules and order. No chaos is allowed in this belief structure; therefore, any deviation from the underlying value is thwarted by the organization and organizational leaders who hold that value. The fact that the current structure has been in place for twenty-seven years gives credence to the perspective that what is in operation has worked, and there is no desire to change it among the state leaders. In addition, the legal belief system, which focuses on power, authority, and control, is operational for the managers in the catchment area and, to some degree, for the current director of mental health and mental retardation.

As long as the organization maintains its current underlying beliefs and values, there is little opportunity for the system to change. In addition, as the organization and its leaders experience stress, the organization will move from a theological belief process to a legal belief system in order to gain control. The managers, conversely, will move to a theological belief system, stating that the organization is violating the rules, and therefore needs to go back to its normal mode of operating to maintain order and control within the system. Thus, the current belief systems are trapping the organization in its desire to change to a new value.

This is a critical issue of understanding for the change process. The underlying assumptions of operation in place within XYZ Corporation are often the issues that organizations and managers face. The issue is this: "I can't make a change if I have the underlying desire to maintain the control that I have always had. Therefore, being incremental is the only avenue that I have if my outcome is to maintain the same types of control that I have had in the past." This becomes the critical issue for the organization in this situation. The concept of living spirit is an anathema to this situation as long as this value set and belief governs operation and decision making. This will therefore become a critical challenge in the intervention.

Although the director and the governor want a change, there has been no assessment to determine that the processes in operation are not achieving the outcomes. In effect, though the outcomes may be achieving the desired results, the discomfort areas are in the process, not the outcomes. Therefore, a critical component of the intervention is in building congruity with the underlying assumptions of the organization and its leaders.

Another issue is in the assessment of the operation value construction of the employees of the organization. If there is a significant difference in the underlying assumptions of the employees, and the assumptions match congruently with the assumptions of the governor and the director, then the organization can begin to look at the development of a strategy for changes based on the area of dissonance existing in the middle of the organization.

The Humanity of the Organization

The nonviolence paradigm is predicated on the belief that humanity is important to organizational and personal effectiveness, and on the assumption that when treatment and valuing people is nonexistent in organizational functioning, violence is the outcome. The recognition of this issue is a driving issue for the organization. Does the organization value its employees? Is there any level of bonding by the organization with the expressed uniqueness of the employee? Is there a process or value in place for hearing and communication that allows employees to participate in the factors that impact their life? Can the individual exist in congruity with the team? Can the organization see its performance based on finding justifiable ends through action, or are the means used validation for the action? These are all questions that get asked in looking at the humanity of the organization and its members.

In the case of XYZ Corporation, humanity is called into question. When the process of creativity and decision making are thwarted by the rules of the organization (theological belief system), then it becomes difficult for a psychological belief system to exist. Tenets of violence, boundaries of violence, structures of violence, vessels of violence, and processes of violence become critical to the potential of the organization to experience and display humanity.

From a consultation perspective, it becomes important to assess the potential of the organization to embrace its soul and treatment of persons with a particular eye to the impacts of organization action irrespective of intent.

The Context Business and Personal Process Paradigms

In the trinity process, two paradigms coexist in the context domain. The business paradigm focuses on the congruity of actions to support or not support concepts of equality, interpretation, reciprocity, empowerment, representation, and commitment. These six dimensions create a sense of wholeness. In the personal paradigm, concepts of discord, emergence, acknowledgment, disclosure, self-indulgence, and re-emergence create a sense of congruence. In looking at the dynamics of XYZ Corporation, there are some important concepts that suggest that there are difficulties in the business and personal processes of the organization.

In the business domain, there are issues that surface initially within the business paradigm. How has the organization responded or reacted to issues of equality for employees or differing areas of the state? Can it be shown through documentation or action that the decisions made ensure that interpretation of the rules are consistent with concepts of equality? Is there a degree of reciprocity in the decision-making process? Are employees empowered, or is the system empowered—making it easy for decisions to be made that offer challenges and opportunities for the system to be responsive to people, communities, and other systems? Are all parties represented in the decision-making process that impacts them? Is there commitment to the issues present in the organization, or does a political process guide the organizational actions?

In the personal domain, equal issues arise in looking at XYZ Corporation. Is there a degree of discord in the personal actions and functioning of the employees of the organization? Are there emerging dynamics like issues of frustration, depression, codependence, anger, sabotage, or union development occurring within the organization? Can the organization or the employees acknowledge the issues arising, or is there too much fear that blocks the effective dialogue of the organization? To what extent is there any disclosure within the organization? Is everyone impacted to the extent that only self-indulgent behavior is occurring? What happens within the organization? Is there compartmentalization on the part of the employees, fragmentation in their strategies? What really happens?

In both domains, has fear taken hold to the extent that a concept of wholeness and congruence are nonexistent terms? Is the process of organizational action such that everyone experiences dynamic paradigm cause-and-effect parameters? What is the nature of the personal and organizational process?

The Development of a Change Strategy

Recognizing the aforementioned issues, it is now possible to begin the dialogue process with management and the employees of the organization. In fact, dialogue is the beginning stage of change. Traditionally, organizations confronted with stagnation have a difficult time embracing the concept of dialogue. Effective, channeled communication is an anathema to the organizational process, so opening the windows to allow dialogue to begin is the first step in the assessment and change process. If you get people to dialogue about the organizational history, process, roles, structure, and outcomes, then you can begin to get the organization to assess their impacts versus their intents.

The data obtained from the dialogue, action forums, or any other communication vehicle will first allow the director of mental health to identify paths that make sense for change versus the development of change in a vacuum. The second reason for the dialogue is to begin the process of dissipating centralized power. In the process paradigms, empowerment for the person and disclosure for the system become critical processes that begin to cut through issues of authority, power, and control.

Next, the strategy for change focuses on the gathering of information around how the organization embraces and responds to the issues of equality and discord, interpretation and emergence, reciprocity and acknowledgment, representation and self-indulgence, and re-emergence and commitment. If these concepts are devoid within the organization, then the assessment of the underlying system or nonsystem becomes key to gathering significant information that can guide a change and development effort.

Finally, all the information is provided to management to begin developing options or scenarios for understanding the system in place. Simultaneously, the process of change would dictate that some attempt be made to establish a communication process with all employees. This perpetuates the empowerment and disclosure process within the organization. Without empowerment and disclosure active in the process of assessment and data analysis, no introduction of the psychological belief system (spirit system) or the aura of calm (humanity system) can be attained.

XYZ Corporation Strategy

The description just given became the process utilized with XYZ Corporation. Remember the importance of empowerment and disclosure from a process perspective, for it becomes a key process. As stated in Chapter 9, this is a process system, so one can start anywhere within the system to ensure that the process paradigms begin to impact the organization. In this case, starting with empowerment and disclosure upon the data-gathering process became important. It should also be noted that during the data-gathering process, two instruments were used to gather information for the trinity process. *The Williams Belief Systems Audit* and *The Organizational Violence Index* were used to gather information to set the stage for the utilization of the empowerment and disclosure paradigm processes.

A general axiom for the development of the strategy is the ability of the organization to learn. Organizational learning is the ability of any organization to gather data and gain insight from its own experience and to alter the manner in which it functions according to the learnings it is experiencing. Two perspectives of this learning are important. First is the reflection-based organization, able to draw from positive, negative, and neutral assessments of its historical action. The second is an experimenting organization, willing to try new thoughts, strategies, and actions to gain insight. Often the ability to change is based on the degree of trauma or dysfunction that is occurring and driving the issues of the organization. In this case, both perspectives are present, making it ripe for the trinity process. Nothing has worked historically. All the experiments and reflections have yielded no positive return, and the frustration levels are high. Key to this issue is the recognition that having order, defining cause and effect, and being flexible with underlying demands for control have all produced unhealthy and unhelpful results for XYZ Corporation. Into that organizational view enters the trinity process.

The Overall Strategy for Change and Development

In meeting with the director of mental health and mental retardation, it became important to frame the issue of change. The key strategy was recognizing that there is no end and no beginning; rather, there are continual processes of change that have milestones along the continuum for improved performance and improved processes, evolving into new directions and new experiences that drive the manner in which service delivery of mental health issues occurs. This is a scary and exciting process of organizational change and development. The transformational nature of this intervention strategy is its influence to always be relevant and important to the deliverers and recipients of the service. The thought of the possibilities was intriguing to the director and to his central office staff. The primary venue for change is both the trinity process and the partnerships created with the four catchment areas and their communities and the political stakeholders who have influenced the system to remain fractured.

The strategy also focused on the assessment of the critical belief systems in operation to help with the framing of a system that mirrors the values of the members of the systems and the milestones that are perceived to be valuable for the long-term future. The strategy looks like the following:

OVERALL CHANGE AND DEVELOPMENT STRATEGY

Assessment of the Current System

Review of the existing policies and procedures

Review of the existing communication vehicles between the four catchment areas and the central office

Review of the existing legislation that defines the framework for regulations and public policy initiatives

Review of documents and reports that identify critical projects and program reporting

Review of current outcomes established by the legislature, the governor, the Mental Health and Mental Retardation Commission, and the existing plan of the office of the director

Interviews with the catchment area community commissions and boards

Interviews with the management team of the organization

Interviews with the key stakeholders (senators, representatives, family members of clients [in-house and outpatient])

Interviews with the last three directors of the mental health–mental retardation organization

Assessment of the Spirit of the Organization

Interviews with all managers of the mental health–mental retardation department

Interviews with all key supervisors of the organization

Interviews with the employees in each program area two levels below the supervisors

Administration of the Belief Systems Audit to all employees of XYZ Corporation

Action forums regarding the results of the Belief Systems Audit and a dialogue about the perceived underlying values of the organization versus the values of the four catchment areas

Assessment of the Humanity of the Organization

Interviews with the employee population of the organization

Interviews with the community leaders

Interviews with the parents of the client population of the organization

Administration of the organizational violence index to all employees of XYZ Corporation

Action forums regarding the results of the organizational violence index, and a dialogue about the underlying assumptions surrounding the treatment and inclusion of employees of the organization—specific attention being given to the potential of the organization to experience the aura of calm

Data Analysis and First Report to the Organization Management

Identification of the instruments used and their purpose in the trinity process

Identification of the underlying assumptions about the organization

Identification of the conflicting paradigms within the organization and the prevailing impact of the conflicting paradigms

Identification of the paradigms in operation from the different stakeholders and influence brokers

Identification of the power dynamics and the reactions to the use of power

Identification of the areas of agreement and congruence

Identification of the areas of disagreement and potential dysfunction

Dialogue meeting with the director of mental health and mental retardation and the four managers of the catchment areas

Identification and Development of a Trinity Plan for Change—The Context-Process Paradigms

Training of identified teams of employees and managers in the trinity process

Understanding of the issues in a tripartate system

Understanding of the concept of process versus ends

Identification of strengths and deficiencies in process management versus causal/end management

Congruence Matching of Mission and Organizational Values

Identification of the organizational mission and guiding principles

Identification of the process paradigm in operation

Explanation with the organizational team of the issues of equality, interpretation, commitment, representation, empowerment, and reciprocity

Identification of the six processes in operation within XYZ Corporation

Identification of the personal-process paradigms in operation

Explanation with the organizational team of the issues of discord, emergence, acknowledgment, disclosure, self-indulgence, and re-emergence

Identification of the six processes in operation within XYZ Corporation

Strategic Business Modeling of XYZ Corporation

Identification of the processes that drive organizational action, with particular attention to the congruence of the organizational processes to the six business-process issues and the six personal-process issues

Examination of the noncongruence on the funding from the legislature, the community, and private organizations for special concerns of the mental health agency

Performance Auditing of XYZ Corporation and Its Impact on the Process Paradigms, Spirit, and Humanity of the Members of the Organization: The Process Paradigm Assessment

The process paradigm assessment looks at the continuum of organizational action versus specific accomplishments geared toward a dedicated service or product—given service delivery in different segments of the organization are not as valued as the congruence and wholeness of *all* the organizational actions to achieve a given milestone on a long-term continuum. How does XYZ Corporation address issues of reciprocity, interpretation, representation, empowerment, equality, and commitment in its internal decision making? What impact do these decisions have on the resources of the organization? Have all the decisions looked at a level of balance with the six processes and the fiscal and human resources of the organization? Are the structures of the organization, as they need to be, based on the processes desired for service delivery? Are the strengths and deficiencies of the organization based on the decisions made, the treatment of staff, and the underlying assumptions of the values that are guiding the organizational process? What impact has public information had on influencing the image and the actions of the organization? Has reciprocity been important or valued in the decision-making process?

Assessing the Gap between What Occurs and What Is Desired: The Trinity Vortex

The trinity vortex is the process of merging the issues of humanity, context, and spirit into an overall strategic and performance plan for the organization. It looks explicitly at areas of opportunities to reframe organizational and personal action on the basis of a changed paradigm. Operating on process continuums versus end-points is essential in this analysis and allows the organization to look at the issues that have occurred historically from a different perspective, thereby creating new strategies and new understandings of shortfalls and shortcomings within the organization. Key to this assessment is identifying the importance of the human condition in the assessment of milestone achievement on a continuum, as well as the performance of the business process paradigm in the choices made by the organization. Essential to this analysis are the initial issues of types of choices addressed. How easy is it to be trapped by the tangents of choice, dynamics of choice, process of choice, and structures of choice in the decision making and milestone development?

The gap identification process also looks at the creation of scenarios for evaluation. What is the best-case scenario, the worst-case scenario, and the middle ground? What degree of risk is assumed in the gap process that has allowed decisions to hit the milestone mark or fall short or exceed? How have employees been brought along in the process of moving from one place in history to another?

What exists for the organization—customers, functions, products, or services? Who impacts the actions of the organization—client groups, politicians, stakeholders, employees, legislators, business groups, or educational institutions? How are we performing the work of the organization—technologies, new technologies, methods that are cost contained, or methods that are bursting the cost goals? What activities are identified within the organization—focus on influence and external impact, or focus on control and internal impact? Is there any balance between the two?

What needs to be addressed as long-term strategies in a process paradigm? Are there milestones to be achieved by changing the structure or by closing various catchments? Should actions be phased, or should the services offered be altered?

The Trinity Contingencies

The trinity process is a process; therefore, multiple strategies are important and impact the commitment and empowerment points in the business process paradigm, and re-emergence and acknowledgment in the personal process, paradigm. Issues of contingency planning that allow the organization to review its membranes that are too easily punctured become important. Where are the vulnerabilities and opportunities for the organization? This includes a hard look at the people and the systems that help or hinder the organizational movement. Which economies impede organizational movement, and which economies help? This is essential to address the different services or businesses that are in operation.

Are there areas of the organization that are functioning exceptionally well that must remain in order to build a constancy in the developmental process of the organization? Where is the survival process of the organization? Where is the transition process of the organization?

All of these strategies help frame the specific actions that are to be taken by the organization as process strategies. Internal vulnerabilities and external vulnerabilities drive the process assessment and the trinity contingency. Looking at the spirit, context, and humanity of the system becomes critical to the assessment. Looking at only one aspect creates voids; looking at the trinity creates wholeness and congruence in the overall movement of the organization.

The Trinity-Implementation Process

The trinity-implementation process operates from the context and humanity components of the trinity system. How people interface with plans and how one assesses the congruence and wholeness of the planning process empowers the effectiveness of the system. Issues of funding, operations, organizational structure, human resource management, and marketing are all impacted from the planning process and are implemented based on the congruity between the human dynamics and the business process. Working on one versus the other causes both to lose in the implementation process. Everything must be worked on simultaneously because the integration between the two is critical. The spirit is the check-and-balance part of the trinity. Congruence with the underlying assumptions and beliefs allows the organization to check the implementation process with the assessment process.

Have leaders of the implementation been chosen because of their legitimate authority or because of their abilities to accomplish the milestones on the continuum? Is there a balance between the organizational process and the functional process? Is there a balance between the functional process and the human process? Is there a constant check and balance between what is desired and what is occurring?

XYZ CORPORATION: WHAT ACTUALLY HAPPENED?

This was a difficult process for XYZ Corporation and its management team. The movement from a causal/end system to a process system is a monumental paradigm shift. The shift is based on reassessing the focus of learning and being, and crafting a paradigm that matches feeling and thoughts with actions and possibilities. XYZ Corporation was experiencing a total systems shift based on desired milestones for the present and the future.

What happened at XYZ Corporation was a change in structure, process, mangerial relationships, and external relationships. XYZ Corporation began to reframe its paradigms and its perspective within the state for the delivery of mental health services.

Organizational Paradigm Shifts

The assessment of organization and personal spirit was by far the most crucial of the assessment processes for this organization. In reviewing their paradigms, it became immediately apparent that the state agency operated from a theological belief system with a legal belief system in times of stress. As the organization had been under stress for a period of six years, the legal belief system was the system of prominence within the organization. Power, authority, and control were the underlying guiding values and assumptions that framed organizational and personal action. Management of the organization found this understanding to be abhorrent. They were mental health professionals who believed in the concept of empowerment and inclusion. How could they operate from systems that created rigidness and one-upmanship over others? The thought of the theological and legal belief systems were anathemas to what they consciously believed. They wanted to operate from the psychological belief system with the legal belief system as backup for the accomplishment of critical budget issues or political issues. This change in focus would, therefore, mean that enormous change would need to be implemented in order to achieve the new underlying assumptions. This would also be difficult because the four managers operated from a legal belief system, and to change would mean to give up their power base.

Enormous time and energy focused on changing the concepts of power and authority to influence and collaboration. Moving from winning to participating and building partnerships that allowed everyone to "have a piece of the action" was difficult. The director of the state agency, therefore, made a pact with the four managers: "Participate in changing the system, and as you change within the process of developing a new system, you maintain your ability to lead the catchment areas—but not control them." This was an interesting pact because continuation of influence was based on a paradigm of change, not a paradigm of constancy.

Six months later, all four managers are leaders of their catchment areas; however, their roles are redefined and framed as catchment facilitators, bringing empowerment and disclosure to the communities to reframe the needs of the communities rather than the needs for the state.

Process Changes for the Present and Future

The process paradigms—the context of change—for the state agency began to develop clarity as the employees of the organization brought new modalities to the process of service delivery. Attention to the issues of reciprocity, interpretation, representation, empowerment, equality, and commitment significantly altered decisions. External and internal dialogue was a key strategy for program planning, community relations, client service delivery, and evaluation of the existing programs. Staff found that as their empowerment factor increased, their value to the organization seemed to increase. The skills they brought to the organization were valued, and the diversity of the staff was its greatest strength rather than its greatest weakness.

As the staff and the community began to evaluate the effectiveness of organizational programs, they began to dialogue about the degree of personal discord they had experienced. Organizational depression began to wane, and the emergence of self and group led to new acknowledgments, disclosures, and self-indulgences. There were some rocky roads, yet there was a check and balance in emerging discord when the self-indulgence got out of hand. This allowed new dialogue moving personal development to areas of re-emergence.

It has been six months and the leaders of the catchment areas are realigning subleaders based on their growth and ability to embrace ideas and ideals rather than fighting the changes that are occurring. The community finds that they are experiencing new levels of empowerment, and the families are taking a stronger role in their treatment of their families, so that reintegration into the society is a real milestone rather than permanent in-hospital stays. Succession planning, tuition reimbursement, and staff development and training have become strong business commitments and strategies for reductions of self-indulgent behavior. Issues of calm are becoming more the norm, with expressed focus on the tenets of violence. Staff intentionally looks at strategies to ensure that everyone is always included, always heard.

Managerial Relationships

There has been a change in the dealings of the managers in their relationships. Focus of the relationship is on the ability to get work accomplished rather than on how to maintain power and control. This has been a monumental change professionally, organizationally, and personally for the managers. Change for the managers focused on their ability to trust the process instead of fearing it.

In interviewing all the managers, their success organizationally had been based on holding the line, not trusting employees, building a power base, and fiercely holding onto power. The trinity process asked them to trust themselves and the employees to create success as a process of growth and development versus control and stricture. Giving up power and authority meant believing that others did not have an agenda to hurt, and if they did, trust the disclosure and discord process to help with the commitment and the empowerment process. This movement took enormous care to be consistent and congruent in personal and organizational actions by all in direct contact with the managers. This was a conscious and intentional act to ensure that "small trust walks" could yield larger trust actions. Within three months, the managers began to let go of the reins and trust that others had good ideas—and that implementation of the ideas would be shared as team-based actions rather than self-indulgent acts.

Eight months have past, and the managers are enjoying the change. Less energy is involved in trusting versus protecting. More minds on an issue are breeding better strategies. Not having to have an end, just a continuation of processes to discover the possibilities for each new thought or ideal, has freed the organization and the managers to embrace the changes in communities. As more changes occur, there has been a stronger move for inclusiveness in the diversity of staff.

Issues of African-American anger have to be reframed to address the expectations that create fear and trepidation in the hearts and minds of the African-Americans who believe they have to be perfect or they will be terminated. The realization of that fear triggered the realization in the managers that there was a commonality that they shared with the minorities: fear of expectations, and that fear's impact on performance, relationships, and trust.

SUMMARY

This has been a wonderful learning journey for the organization and for me as the consultant. That is the strength of the trinity process. Everyone is a co-learner with everyone else. Everyone is accountable for their own business commitment and their own personal empowerment in the context paradigms. Everyone is accountable for their collaboration in the development of spirit paradigms. What one values and believes often drives how one looks at the world and shapes their performance in that worldview. Everyone is accountable for their adherence to the humanity and nonviolence paradigm. Everyone is accountable for their disclosure and participation in the equality of decisions and the representation of personal and professional action in the seeking of wholeness. Everyone is accountable for managing their self-indulgence. Everyone is accountable for operating holistically rather than in compartmentalized and fragmented ways.

This is a system of movement. Nothing is static, and nothing has an end. Only movement and embracing of movement frees the person and the organization to understand and accept difference, newness, diversity, and change. It is a journey on a broad path, able to shift with new information that suggests that shifting is appropriate for achievement of needed milestones. Every movement has meaning, purpose, opportunities, and vulnerabilities. Embracing the challenges is the challenge of the trinity process.

EPILOGUE

Coming Full Circle: The Trinity Process Revisited

The creation of a practical and theoretical process for personal and organizational development is a difficult process. An underlying assumption of this process is the concept of living for people and business systems. The creation of an endless paradigm system has been a long-time dream. As I have grown personally and professionally, I have discovered that nothing ends and nothing begins; rather, there is this process of development that allows me to look at the history, present, and future, recognizing that what I experience and understand is continually based on the choices that I make—choices that I make based on my personal development and my organizational experiences, choices that are sometimes made for me by the choices that others make because of their experiences. The choices drive so much of the learning possibilities.

This is a book of choices and learnings. Transformation and learning involves the risk of change in order to grow. Businesses fail because they are unwilling or unable to transform. People become stunted because they fear changing and transforming. Societies fail because control, power, and authority become the underlying assumptions for thought, action, and process. Each person, group, organization, and society has its holocaust, and in that holocaust; we make choices for how we frame and react to the present and the future. Businesses have taken the holocaust and killed their spirit and humanity, in fear of losing control and power. People have taken their holocaust experiences and chosen to freeze themselves with historical tapes that frame their thinking and action for the present and the future. This book is about looking at that holocaust and processing that experience as a process of transformation, learning, and being. This is strength of the trinity. No power on earth can inhibit one's desire to learn, change, grow, and transform except the fear within. Therefore, trusting, belonging, growing, and being become the anchors of learning and growing.

Humanity, context, and spirit frame how we look at issues of personal and organizational psychosis. Humanity, context, and spirit frame how we understand our manic behavior and our depressive behavior. Humanity, context, and spirit frame how we understand our personal and organizational codependence. Humanity, context, and spirit frame how we embrace ourselves and our experiences within business. The trinity is a process of change that challenges each of us to think critically about who we are, what we do, how we interface with others, how we embrace life's experiences, and how we explain the changes that occur in our lives. It is never about ends, only changes. It is never about beginnings, only processes. It is never about control, only influence. It is never about me or you; rather, it is about us. There is never a them, there is only us. We are ourselves, and we are them.

Recently I was listening to an organizational leader talking about his organization's ability to change and reframe its present to craft a different future. The organization had decided that it wanted to craft a new future based on a product that it believed would change the computer support industry. He was energetic, excited, and firmly believed in the path that his organization had chosen. After the presentation, he was in the hallway talking with some other executives and stated, "We whipped our employees into shape and put the fear of God in them to do things the way we want." I was saddened by his comments because I recognized that the changes of the products for the future maintained a human strategy of the past. In the noncongruence of the actions, the organizational paradigm was not about equality, reciprocity, or representation. The actions were not about empowerment. The actions would not foster emergence, acknowledgment, disclosure, or congruence; rather, the actions would only create organizational violence and dysfunction. The sadness of his statements is the sadness of the future of business.

Our futures are based on our embracing the tripartite system, not linear or dualistic thought as discussed in Chapter 9 of this book. Our futures are based on embracing the full spectrum of who we are and what we can become, not what we have. Sometimes I want to suggest that we throw away our histories to create our futures, yet I recognize that our histories help frame who we are. I have come to the realization that we can always revisit and reframe how we have looked at our histories and presents to make a difference in how we choose our futures. This is the challenge of the trinity process for the individual, group, and system.

Ann Wilson Schaef and Diane Fassel said in their book, *The Addictive Organization*, "Addictive organizations are hurting organizations. They are in trouble internally. They are not evil and vicious groups, although they may do things that are personally and socially destructive. The addictive organization and the individual need to recover." This is a book about recovery through reframing personal and organizational choice.

As a person of African descent, I am reminded of a tradition in African culture that speaks of healing through storytelling. I am intrigued by that process. As a consultant, I constantly listen to the stories of businesses and people as they try to speak to the pains and traumas that have framed their current behavior in organizations. As a professor, I listen to students tell their stories about what drives them and brings them to the unique program at the California Institute of Integral Studies. As a father, I listen to my sons tell their stories of new experiences that are shaping their choices for their lives, and I marvel at the power of stories to heal the pains and hurts that drive personal and organizational action. I decided it would be appropriate to tell you a story as a milestone in this book. The story is about development, pain, trauma, and transformative learning that shaped a person and a business using the trinity process.

THE STORY OF ONE, THE STORY OF MANY

Jacqui is perusing her life. She is the senior executive officer of Mariah Corporation, a multinational agriculture firm specializing in helping developing countries in South America repair their forests. She has been with the firm for ten years, working diligently from the position of management analyst to senior vice president of research and program development. Recently, she was accosted on the street by a homeless man. He said, "I know you! We went to school together at the University of Oklahoma majoring in Agricultural Economics. Help me, please!" Jacqui was taken aback by the actions of the homeless man. She was shocked, appalled, scared, saddened, sympathetic, and questioning of the feelings she was having in seeing this down-trodden man.

Jacqui asked the man named David if he would like to get something to eat, and he responded yes. They went to the closest diner to get a little respite from the elements. It was a cold day in Chicago. As they ate and talked, Jacqui heard this tale from David.

"Jacqui, I am so ashamed. I graduated with you and went to work for MARKCORP, an agricultural conglomerate in Idaho. I was doing well. I went into the firm as a management analyst and worked my way up to senior vice president within four years. I felt I was doing a great job. I focused on the numbers and the products and we were beginning to really make profits." Jacqui said, "What happened?" David responded, "I am not sure. I know that I was sort of tough in the decision-making process. I cut corners, slashed staff, and changed the relationships of people who worked in company to meet the needs that I had to gain more profits. I mean, the schools that we went to told us this was the way to succeed. I did all the things I was trained to do, and it was going well. About three years ago, the chief executive officer decided that he would restructure the organization. He did a climate survey among the employees of the organization and discovered that the climate of the organization was poor, and that it was based on the way people were treated. That was my area. I guess in my attempt to meet the performance goals of the organization, I beat up on people and was pretty ruthless."

Jacqui said, "You mean, you did what they wanted, and then they terminated you because you were good at what you did?" David said, "You got it!" David shared with Jacqui that he had applied for positions all around the country. After 450 applications, and numerous job interviews and networking activities, nothing positive had occurred. The money ran out—he lost the house, car, and memberships—and no one continued to speak with him. He was alone, and he felt it was his own doing. If he got another chance, he would be different, because the impact on him was devastating.

David and Jacqui continued to talk as they ate together for the first time in ten years. Jacqui discovered that David had been really successful, commanding a salary of $200,000 per year with bonus options that yielded the potential for $500,000 of bonus money. He had never married, and had lived the life he felt he was supposed to lead. He had purchased a million-dollar home in the country club, drove a new 600S series Mercedes, belonged to the "right organizations," and all the other trappings that are supposed to come with success. When the climate survey was finalized, the chief executive officer felt that it was easier to terminate David and start fresh than to save him for the actions he had taken over time. As they continued to talk, they talked of options for David—with the promise from Jacqui that she would see if there were some way that she could help him. She believed this was an appropriate thing to do. She helped him find a small hotel and gave him some money. They parted company, promising to get together within the next two weeks.

Jacqui is now in her office. She recognizes that some of the behaviors of David are her behaviors. She, too, rose quickly within the organization and has periodically acted as he had to get where she has gotten. She says to herself, "I have got to change. I don't want to end up like

David! There has got to be a better way!" Jacqui recognized that she had been ruthless. In fact, that was the way the educational process had functioned. She was doing things the way she had learned. It had positive payoffs. She did not believe the things that had happened to David would happen to her; however, it was possible. He had been smarter than she was and had gotten the better positions.

Jacqui determined that she must protect herself from that behavior and begin to make a change. Where do I start? What are my issues? How will I know that what I am doing is good for me and the company? Is the history of this company so strong that I cannot alter it? What about my image? How will I change my image and my style so that what happened to David does not happen to me? These questions and many others began to plague Jacqui. She went to the human resources department to gather information. Was absenteeism high? Was sick leave high? Were there lots of grievances? Were people leaving the organization left and right? What were the data she could use to make decisions for the future? The human resources area of the company told her, "We are having some retention and management-oriented problems, nothing out of the ordinary!"

Jacqui breathed a sigh of relief. She felt she was safe and, over time, forgot the thoughts and went back to the patterns that she had originally operated from in the past. During the next year, Jacqui continued with her patterns of managing. She cut people off and "storm-troopered" over people who did not make the same decisions she did. She disempowered employees. She made business decisions that drove up profits but wiped out people. She was, in her mind, being successful. As her gauge, she would check monthly with human resources to see how things were going. As long as the data did not change, she felt that she was okay.

Another year passed, and the CEO of Mariah Corporation called her in and said, "Jacqui, it's just not working out! Over the past two years, complaints have come into my office about your heavy-handed approach to managing people. I have even had a complaint from one of our clients in South America about your behavior. This is just not working, and I need to restructure and cut my losses. You are terminated from employment here, effective immediately!"

Jacqui was floored. She did not know what to think about the actions that were occurring. She wanted to ask for another chance. She could change. She could make a difference in the decisions. What about all the profits she had brought into the company? Didn't that count for another chance?

Jacqui is at home in the window seat of her house. She thinks of David and wonders why she did not take the clue that she had seen in their short meeting. She wondered about her arrogance and the impact it had on her and, now, the actions of others. She wondered about the concept of choice. She wondered about her future and present. Could she survive? Would she end up like David if it took forever to get another job? She was not young any longer. She was a forty-five-year-old executive. She had not saved to the same extent as David because her salary was not as high. Could she make it? Could she see it through to the end?

THOUGHTS ON THE STORY OF ONE, THE STORY OF MANY

The story of Jacqui is not a foreign one, for it occurs daily in the lives of business and people. The issue of the story, and the issue for business, is the choice process that so often occurs when we compartmentalize our actions and thoughts about behavior and impact. Irrespective to our intents, we are always accountable for our impacts. Jacqui and David have paid a high price for their choices. They have continued to pay based on their inability or unwillingness to blend the issues of humanity, spirit, and context in their choices.

We each pay for the same reasons. We did not come to this world omnipotent and "all-knowing." We did not come to this world with the answers. We did not come to this world being self-assured that our choices would last forever. Therefore, our choices impact and alter the course of events. To look at that process as a casual effect with clearly defined ends sets the stage for us losing and paying costs that are not helpful for the person or the system.

Jacqui and David represent the norm of modern business and business professionals. Jacqui and David represent the failure of humanity to confront its choices and craft futures that empower and collaborate with others rather than control and disempower others. Jacqui and David represent the arrogance of business and society in its intentional valuing of power, control, and authority. The choices for the future and the choices for the present that focus on blending, sharing, caring, being, and belonging seem to make a difference that allows us to move with the future in partnership with others.

The trinity process focuses on our potential to move forward with the belief that we, like everything, change. The trinity process focuses on decision making based on values and beliefs. The trinity process focuses on change and congruity based on the humanity and inclusion of people and ideals. The trinity process focuses on the capacity of systems and people to intentionally and thoughtfully make decisions based on the wholeness and congruity of the decision and its long-reaching impacts that are process focused, not end focused. As long as we look at change as a process rather than a product or an end, we maintain the capacity to embrace and flow with the change.

SUMMARY

Futures are made and destroyed because of the underlying assumptions that frame that future. I believe business and human futures are best framed in the capacity to change, grow, learn, and transform. Businesses live because of that transformation. So do we.

CLASSIFIED
BIBLIOGRAPHY

BOOKS

Abraham, F. D. *A Visual Introduction to Dynamical Systems Theory for Psychology.* Santa Cruz, Calif.: Aerial Press, 1990.

Bateson, G. *Steps to an Ecology of Mind.* New York: Ballantine Books, 1988.

Beattie, Melody. *Codependent No More.* Minneapolis: Harper/Hazelden, 1987.

Bohm, D. *Wholeness and the Implicate Order.* London: Routledge and Kegan Paul, 1980.

Brookfield, Stephen D. *Developing Critical Thinkers: Challenging Adults to Explore Alternative Ways of Thinking and Acting.* San Francisco: Jossey-Bass, 1987.

Buber, Martin. *I and Thou.* New York; Insel-Verlag, Corp. Macmillan Company, 1923.

Capra, F. *The Turning Point.* New York: Bantam Books, 1987.

Covey, Stephen R. *The Seven Habits of Highly Effective People.* New York: Simon and Schuster, 1989.

Deal, Terrence, and Kennedy, Allan. *Corporate Cultures: The Rites and Rituals of Corporate Life.* Reading, Mass.: Addison-Wesley Publishing Company, 1982.

Freire, Paulo. *Pedagogy of the Oppressed.* New York: Seabury Press, 1973.

Gibb, Jack. *Trust: A New View of Personal and Organizational Development.* Los Angeles: Guild of Tutors Press, 1978.

Gustafson, Katharine. *Drug and Alcohol Testing for Local Government Transportation Employees: The Public Employer's Guide.* Washington, D.C.: International City/County Management Association, Shaw, Pittman, Potts & Trowbridge, 1995.

Haley, Jay. *Uncommon Therapy.* New York: The Norton Library, 1973.

Hersey, Paul, and Blanchard, Ken. *Management of Organizational Behavior: Utilizing Human Resources.* 4th ed. Englewood Cliffs, N.J.: Prentice-Hall, 1982.

Jackson, John H., and Morgan, Cyril P. *Organizational Theory: A Macro Perspective for Management.* 2nd ed. Englewood Cliffs, N.J.: Prentice-Hall, 1982.

Katz, Daniel, and Kahn, Robert. *Social Psychology of Organizations.* New York: John Wiley, 1966.

Laszlo, E. *Evolution: The Grand Synthesis*. Boston: Shambala, 1987.

Mezirow, Jack. *Transformative Dimensions of Adult Learning*. San Francisco: Jossey-Bass, 1991.

McWhinney, Will. *Paradigms and Systems Theories*. Santa Barbara, Calif.: Specialty Books, 1991.

Pritchett, Price, and Pound, Ron. *High Velocity Culture Change: A Handbook for Managers*. Dallas: Pritchett & Associates, 1994.

Robey, Daniel, and Altman, Steven. *Organization Development: Progress and Perspectives*. New York: Macmillan, 1982.

Rokeach, Milton. *Beliefs, Attitudes, and Values: A Theory of Organization and Change*. San Francisco: Jossey Bass, 1968.

Schaef, Anne Wilson, and Fassel, Diane. *The Addictive Organization*. Cambridge, Mass.: Harper and Row, 1988.

Senge, Peter. *The Fifth Discipline*. Boston: MIT Press, 1994.

Srivastva, Suresh, and Cooperrider, David. *Appreciative Management and Leadership*. San Francisco: Jossey-Bass, 1990.

Thomlinson, Ralph. *Sociological Concepts and Research: Acquisition, Analysis, and Interpretation of Social Information*. New York: Random House, 1965.

Venerable, Grant. *The Paradox of the Silicon Savior: Charting the Reformation of the High Tech Super State*. San Francisco: MVM Productions, 1987.

Watson, Robert I. *The Great Psychologists*. 4th ed. Philadelphia: J. B. Lippincott Company, 1978.

Williams, Janet B. *Diagnostic and Statistical Manual of Mental Disorders*. Rev. 3rd ed. Philadelphia: American Psychiatric Association, 1987.

Williams, Lloyd C. *The Congruence of People and Organizations: Healing Dysfunction from Inside-Out*. Westport, Conn.: Quorum Books, 1993.

Williams, Lloyd C. *The Williams Belief Systems Audit*. Westport, Conn.: Quorum Books, 1993.

Williams, Lloyd C. *Organizational Violence: Creating a Prescription for Change*. Westport, Conn.: Quorum Books, 1994.

Williams, Lloyd C. *The Organizational Violence Index*. Westport, Conn.: Quorum Books, 1994.

ARTICLES

Coopers & Lybrand. "The Strategic Impact of Human Resources: Building High Performance Work Systems." H. R. Advisory, Coopers & Lybrand, San Francisco: June 1995.

Dell, P. F. "Beyond Homeostasis: Towards a Concept of Coherence." *Family Process* 21 (1; 1982): 21–42.

Kublius, Vince, and Courion, Jeffrey. "The Flaw in the Ointment." *O. D. Practitioner* 26 (3 & 4). Pelham, N.Y.: O. D. Network, 1994.

Pettit & Martin. "Drug Free Workplace Seminar." San Francisco: Price-Waterhouse, 1990.

Smith Kline Beecham Clinical Laboratories: "Depression in the Workplace." *Balanced Health Report*, Vol. 3, No. 2. Smith Kline Beecham Laboratories, Collegeville, Pa., 1995.

JOURNALS REVIEWED

Behavioral Science (no specific articles)
International Journal of General Systems (no specific articles)

INDEX

ABOUT THE AUTHOR

LLOYD C. WILLIAMS is an Associate Professor of Business in the Masters of Arts in Business and the Masters of Arts in Organizational Development and Transformation Programs at the California Institute of Integral Studies, San Francisco. He is also President of The Williams Group, an Oakland, California, consulting firm specializing in organizational change and development with clients in the public and private sectors throughout the United States. Dr. Williams holds advanced degrees in psychology and theology and is the author of three previous Quorum books: *The Congruence of People and Organizations* (1993), *Organizational Violence* (1994), and *Human Resources in a Changing Society* (1995).